For happier sewing!

Emina Darmo

To Judy
from Mim
, 1982

IT'S SEW SIMPLE

IT'S SEW SIMPLE
By Eunice Farmer

Features Press
Indianapolis, Indiana 46220

ACKNOWLEDGMENTS

"My love affair with fabrics and design,
created my career. My wanting to share
this love, created a teacher. My students
and my readers, continue to create my inspiration."

A special thank-you to everyone who has had
a part in making sewing a happy adventure for me!

Contents

1 Sewing Tips

Easy Skirt Marker; Organized Sewing; School Picture; Neater Sewing Room; Notches for Accuracy; Prevent Popping Buttons; Disposable Press Cloth; Front and Back; Matching Plaid; Collar Stays; Fix Snags; Needle Size; Use of Old Slips; Portable Sewing; Pressing Seams; Close the Facing; Knicker Look; Reinforce Pockets; Easy Sliding; Two-Piece Waistband; Holding Fabrics; Seam Shortcut; Fabric Guide; Lint-Free Fake Fur; Stabilizing Buttonholes; Pattern Filing; Storing Small Articles; Nonroll Waistline; Attaching Interfacing; Fabrics on Hand; Quick Belt Loops; Zigzag Cut; Denim Book Covers; Prevent Needles Breaking; Strawberry Patches; Extra Seam Tape; Easy Waistline Casings; Wrap Skirt Finishing; Buttonholes on Wraparounds; Sleeve Board Cover; Clean Machine; Crisp Look; Trace on Interfacing; Fuse the Hem; Threading a Needle; Kitchen Tip; Smooth Pocket Edge; Avoid Loose Threads; Cover a Stain on Sweater and Dress; Interfacing Tip; Right and Wrong Side; Covered Buttons; Handy for Pressing; Machine Cover; Creases; Measuring Hems; School Clothes; Prevent Damage to Fabric; Caution; Velcro® for Babies' Outfits; Reinforce Buttons; Knit Blanket Binding; Invisible Thread; Handy Bobbins; Easy Zipper; Easy Needle Threading; Pattern Tape; Press Crease; Anchor Metal Buttons; Pressing Tip; Pins for Nylon Net; Perfect Curves; Shortening Sleeves; No-Slip Patch Pockets; Plastic Shirt Stays; Quick Jacket Lining; Turning Belts; Needle Threader; Pocket Shaper; Prevent Button Damage; Signed Quilt; Which Needle Is Which?

2 Not for Beginners Only

Right Age for Sewing; Starting Right; Tips for Beginners; Adult Beginner; Try Sewing; Beginning Fitting; Sewing Straight; Straight Seams; Sewing Errors

3 Good Sewing Machines Make Happy Sewers

Make a Needle Pad; Use Correct Needle; How to Love Your New Sewing Machine; Keep the Needle in High Position; Skipped Stitches; Sewing Fine Knit; Puckered Seams; Sewing Machine Gift

Chapter 1
SEWING TIPS

Easy Skirt Marker

If you don't own a skirt marker, a sink plunger serves nicely as a marking guide for pinning garment hems on a person or a dress form. It will stand alone on the floor and leave both hands free for pinning. Mark the desired length of skirt on the plunger handle with chalk; then move the plunger around the skirt as you pin up the hem!

Organized Sewing

Plan to do your cutting of several garments at the same time. Purchase large, plastic dish pans which stack, and place all the cut pieces, your pattern, thread, and zippers all together in the plastic pan. Whenever you decide to work on any garment, simply get out the pan with the complete fabric and findings. You don't have to sort and hunt for anything.

School Picture

Mothers who sew usually make children's school clothes. When they wear something special for their school pictures, save the scraps of fabric and cover the frame of the picture so it matches the outfit. It's darling!

Neater Sewing Room

Here's a tip to keeping the sewing area a little neater. Buy a child's brightly colored plastic play broom to sweep up the scraps and threads around the sewing machine. This brightly colored toy broom isn't out of place and conspicuous propped in the sewing room, and it is always within reach.

Notches for Accuracy

This little tip is very helpful for beginners. Get in the habit of using a very small notch or clip to mark the center fronts and backs, folds of facings, shoulder mark on sleeves, and also the two lines for the ends of darts. It saves time and you have instant matching for accuracy. Be sure your clips aren't too deep.

Prevent Popping Buttons

When your dress or robe buttons all the way down the front to the hem, sew on the last several buttons with elastic thread. This will prevent them from popping off because of the extra strain when sitting or walking.

Disposable Press Cloth

When using fusible interfacing, two wet paper towels, squeezed and spread over the area to be fused, form an excellent press cloth. Imagine, a disposable press cloth.

Front and Back

When making a skirt or pants with an elastic waistband, and especially those you make for children, sew a small square in the back of the garment at the center. Instantly, you can see which is the front or back.

Matching Plaid

When you are making a true-bias skirt, one piece front and one piece back and cut singly with the right side up, cut one piece first (usually the front); then, leaving the tissue pattern pinned to the fabric, turn it over onto the other tissue pattern (back) and fabric. You can position the plaid lines to match.

Collar Stays

Instead of putting stays in the collars of a shirt like the ready-made ones, use fusible interfacing and put the stay between the undercollar and the interfacing and fuse in place. It stays put and doesn't show. Next, complete the collar as directed.

Fix Snags

When you get a snag in a knit garment, take a needle threader and insert the tip through the hole from the wrong side of the knit. Put the snagged thread through the wire loop and pull it to the wrong side. This makes the snag go through the hole it was pulled from, and it becomes almost invisible.

Needle Size

When trying to find the right size needle for your sewing machine and finding it difficult to read the size on the needle (even with a magnifying glass), rub colored chalk over the printing on the needle. The size will be much easier to read.

Use of Old Slips

The new loose tops we are all wearing are sometimes too cool without a T top, but too warm with it. I came up with an idea that works perfectly for me. Cut a too-short slip and wear it as an underwear top over a bra. Tuck it into your slacks. It's a good way to make use of slips that can't be lengthened.

Portable Sewing

A portable sewing machine is often a bother to get out and carry to the kitchen table to sew. A portable TV cart allows you to make only one trip. The sewing machine fits on the top shelf and other supplies fit on the lower shelf. It's easy to keep all sewing and mending up to date.

Pressing Seams

Sewers should press seams open before trimming, no matter what the directions say. It is infinitely easier to press open a standard seam width than one that has been trimmed to ¼ inch. Always notch or clip the curved seams first; then trim the required amount and renotch if necessary!

Close the Facing

To keep the unstitched facing flap closed on the wraparound skirts, iron carefully on both sides. Open the flap (facing) and spray INSIDE with spray starch. Close flap and iron again on both sides for instant fusing. Great!

Knicker Look

If you have slacks in your closet that are too short and if you live where you can wear boots, just tuck them into the boots. Presto! You have a knicker look and it hasn't cost you a cent.

Reinforce Pockets

When making pockets in the side seams of a garment, the back seam must be slashed to allow the pocket to fold to the front. In order to prevent this weakened area from pulling out, press a small iron-on patch over it before stitching.

Easy Sliding

Try using the lead from a pencil on a zipper which becomes stubborn. Just run the lead up and down the zipper. The graphite does the trick and the zipper will slide easily again.

Two-Piece Waistband

When making ladies' slacks or skirts, make the waistband in two pieces (with a seam at the center back). Connect both pieces to each section of the slacks or skirt; then sew center back seam all in one. It's just like ready-made men's trousers. This makes altering much easier after a few extra pounds creep up or after a lucky weight loss.

Holding Fabrics

A corsage pin or very large needle is handy for holding fabric as it feeds under the presser foot, especially those crawly fabrics. Also, it is perfect for adjusting gathers just before they go under the presser foot. Keep one next to your sewing machine at all times, and you'll be surprised how often you will put it to good use.

Seam Shortcut

For a shortcut on French seams, sew a regular ⅝-inch seam on the wrong side, press both seams together to one side, and then machine stitch about ¼ inch from the first stitching through all three layers.

Trim off the excess fabric, turn to the right side and there's a seam with a double stitching (much like a flat-felled seam) that will never pull out. It's perfect for any type of sportswear.

Fabric Guide

Keep a large piece of regular interfacing that is sixty inches wide. Mark it in several widths—fifty-four, forty-five and thirty-six inches. Mark lines in the opposite direction every half-yard. If your fabric is going to be very expensive, purchase the pattern and place it on the guide. You would be surprised how often you can save anywhere from 1/3 to 1/2 yard of fabric by carefully arranging the pattern pieces on the fabric.

Lint-Free Fake Fur

When working with fake fur, put all the cut pieces in your clothes dryer on air cycle to fluff. This gets rid of all that loose fur and saves time and tempers when cleaning around your sewing area. It also avoids excess lint getting into your sewing machine mechanism.

Stabilizing Buttonholes

Before making machine buttonholes on knit fabrics, place a piece of double-sided bonding gauze (Stich Witchery) slightly larger than the buttonhole between the outer garment and the interfacing. Make buttonholes and then steam press. When buttonholes are cut open, there will be no feathery threads showing. Also, stretching will be substantially reduced.

Pattern Filing

It is always hard to fold patterns after use and get them back into the original pattern envelope. I cut the front of the pattern envelope out and tape it to the front of a medium-size manila envelope. The folded pattern and the back of the pattern envelope go into the folder. They are stored in a metal file for easy reference and the pattern itself is not such a mess.

Storing Small Articles

To store my small sewing articles, I save leftover potato chip cans. Cover the cans with contact paper which matches your sewing room, and label each. You can even buy a wine rack to store the cans on.

Nonroll Waistline

To keep the elastic from curling on slacks or skirts at the waistline (including the nonroll elastic which also curls at times), machine stitch through the elastic and the fabric vertically at about four points of the waistline, both sides, front and back. This should be done after the gathers have been evenly spaced the way you want them permanently. The machine stitching will never show, and you'll love the results.

Attaching Interfacing

When making a jacket with interfacing down the fronts and darts at the bustline or any shaping, the instructions are always to stitch the darts first and then baste the interfacing in place. You are now dealing with a curved section of your jacket. The reverse procedure is easier. Attach the interfacing first while the fronts are still flat; then put the darts or other construction in second. Your garment will never be stretched out of shape.

Fabrics on Hand

Buy a small wallet or makeup bag and each time you make a new garment, add a small piece of the fabric. You never know when you're shopping how often you will find just the right accessory or need to match the color of your fabric. It's marvelous to always have it at your fingertips.

Quick Belt Loops

To make belt loops in a hurry, cut twice the desired width, fold both side edges to the center, and fuse layers together. This method leaves no bulky seams, no sewing, no tedious turning to the right side, and no edges that ravel.

Zigzag Cut

When cutting a pattern apart to add more material, do an uneven zigzag cut so the parts can be fitted together again like a jigsaw puzzle, should they become separated.

Denim Book Covers

Every year when children begin school, their books need covers. Before you know it, they are in shreds and need to be done again. Use blue denim fabric, and the books will not need recovering for a year. They are a real hit with the teachers and the other students as well.

Make them the same as paper covers; however, stitch the top and bottom edges to fit snugly over the book, and then turn right side out.

Before completing the stitching, you may wish to do machine embroidery, hand embroidery or attach favorite patches for identification as well as novelty.

Prevent Needles Breaking

When sewing canvas or any heavy, closely woven fabric, run a bar of soap over the seamline before stitching. The needle will enter the heavy fabric easier, and it won't break as easily.

Strawberry Patches

Instead of putting unsightly patches on pants, dungarees or T-shirts, use appliques. Sew fruits, animals, flowers, or whatever on children's clothes. It's fun and delights the children.

Extra Seam Tape

When applying seam tape or lace binding at the edge of hems, take a one-inch tuck in the binding at each side seam. This way, when you want to let out the seam, there will be enough binding to match across the added hem edge so you won't have to piece the binding.

Easy Waistline Casings

When a pattern calls for making a waistline casing for either elastic or a drawstring, it's difficult to cross a seam. The seam usually pushes to one side of the seam allowance, preventing easy insertion of the elastic or drawstring.

To prevent this, iron a narrow strip of Stitch Witchery, double the length of the casing, onto both sides of the seam allowance. This keeps the seam permanently flat and smooth, facilitating the passage of elastic with ease. This tip could apply to a casing in any area of your garments.

Fig. 1 – Wrap Skirt

Wrap Skirt Finishing

When finishing a wraparound skirt, sew a large hook at the waistline of the part that laps. Try the skirt on and hold the waistline snug. Mark and sew on an eyelet. This keeps the skirt from sagging and helps prevent the small opening through which the belt slides from tearing out.

Buttonholes on Wraparounds

When making a wrap skirt that requires a buttonhole at each side for the ties to go through, sew your buttonhole on an angle instead of vertically. The tie will go through the buttonhole with ease, and it will last longer and not pull out of shape. Also, to accommodate the width of the tie if fabric is heavy, you can make a larger buttonhole by slanting it.

Sleeve Board Cover

My built-in ironing board has a small sleeve board that needs a new cover, and since they don't seem to sell such an item, I bought a pair of tube socks with lots of stretch. They are a perfect shape for the small board. The socks are quite heavy, so you need use only one. Keep the other for a spare for the future. It works perfectly.

Clean Machine

My sewing machine gathers a lot of lint around the bobbin area. To clean it, I cleaned an old mascara brush with dishwashing detergent and used the brush on the machine.

Crisp Look

A yardstick is just the right width to slide into those long ties for pressing. It's an easy way to get a neat, crisp look to those hard-to-reach spots.

Trace on Interfacing

Perfect points and curves can be achieved every time when making a collar band if a tracing is made on the interfacing from the pattern before the interfacing is attached to the collar fabric. You'll have perfect guidelines for your machine stitching.

Fuse the Hem

To keep from catching your heels in the hems of long dresses, use Stitch Witchery instead of sewing the hem by hand. Your heels will never catch again—what joy!

Threading a Needle

For anyone who has a hard time threading a needle and has lots of basting to do while making a garment, tape a needle threader to your sewing machine with the head wire sticking up. Simply cap the needle over it, turn and pull thread through.

Kitchen Tip

Here's a kitchen tip that we can all do in a second with our sewing machines. Machine stitch a circle in the center of your pastry cloth the size of the pie pan you use most (or mark two sizes). The stitching will serve as a handy guide when rolling out your pastry dough.

Smooth Pocket Edge

When making a pocket of lightweight fabric that is to be topstitched to a garment, cut it double and stitch it all around the outside edge.

For turning, make a slit in the center of one side big enough to turn the pocket right side out. Clip corners before turning. By pressing on smoothly and sealing the slit with a scrap of bonding material, you'll have a nice smooth edge on all your pockets every time.

Avoid Loose Threads

To avoid loose threads at the ends of decorative tucks or darts, rethread your sewing machine. Bring the bobbin thread up through the needle and continue through all the guides, tension wheel, etc., leaving some thread extended at the top where your spool of thread would normally be placed. Begin your stitching at the end of the tuck or dart and continue to the seamline. You must rethread the machine for each tuck, but you will avoid tying those loose threads on each one.

Cover a Stain on Sweater and Dress

Purchase a skein of contrasting acrylic yarn and work a large cross-stitch design down the front of the sweater on either side. The same design can be applied to the dress. You are able to cover the stains completely, maintain a beautiful feminine look, and best of all, you are able to continue to wear the garments. Rescue garments by adding a touch of trim or embroidery.

Interfacing Tip

Place lightweight interfacing OVER the paper pattern and trace the seamlines after referring to the construction guide. This eliminates wasted interfacing and the time it takes to trim each piece after it is cut.

Right and Wrong Side

Many of our new and lovely materials look very nearly alike on both sides. To prevent sewing a piece wrong side up, apply a small piece of transparent tape to the wrong side of each piece of cut material as soon as you unpin the pattern. The tape pulls off as you use each piece and leaves the material undamaged. One quick look to find the piece of tape immediately tells you that's the wrong side of your material.

Covered Buttons

Small buttons such as those used on wedding gowns are usually difficult to cover with slippery fabric. Hand sew a row of stitching near the outer edge of the cut circle of fabric; then pull the thread over the button until it fits fairly snugly around the top of the button frame. Hold securely with a few stitches and proceed to put the back of the button frame on as the package instructions suggest.

Handy for Pressing

Set up a sturdy child's ironing board, well padded, beside your sewing machine. The iron is always on beside it (you can switch it off and on as needed). If pressing is this handy, you are never tempted to forego this all-important step.

Machine Cover

Slip a cotton pillow slip over the leaf of your console sewing machine. It's a fabulous aid when sewing slithery fabrics such as Qiana®, chiffons and jerseys, because it controls the fabric being fed through the machine. Also, it protects the fabric from snagging on hinges and hardware.

Creases

When making men's trousers, as well as my own, I always press the creases in immediately after cutting the pieces of fabric. It's much easier before assembling the pants and the creases are always in the right place.

Measuring Hems

Here's a great way to do hems when there's no one to help.

Place a wide rubber band on your leg where you would like your dress to end. If you are working on an unfinished dress, put a second rubber band where the fabric ends. The distance between the bands is the amount you shorten the dress. The procedure can be reversed to lengthen dresses.

School Clothes

When children start school, the weather is still warm and short sleeves are in order. When the cooler weather comes, they need long sleeves. Purchase a little extra fabric for an extra set of shirt sleeves. Insert the short sleeves; later, remove and add the long sleeves. Incidentally, make the long sleeves immediately and keep them in the laundry room. Wash them each time with the shirt, and the colors will match when the long sleeves are inserted.

Prevent Damage to Fabric

To prevent damaging the fabric with the teeth of the buttonhole attachment, slip the window of clear plastic from a zipper package over the fabric. You will be able to see exactly where to line up your needle to begin the buttonhole.

Caution

A word of caution is to preshrink ANYTHING that will be washed later. If you intend throwing it in the dryer, be sure to do the same to your fabric before cutting the garment.

If you are adding trims or braids or cotton lace of any type, be sure to preshrink that also. Some women even suggest preshrinking the zippers.

If you purchase cotton knits that are tube-shaped when you buy them, be sure to refold the creased edges before cutting, as they may leave permanent creases at the center front and back of your garment if you don't.

When purchasing buttons, be sure they are washable.

Dark colors will continue to bleed when washed, so be sure to wash them separately. Don't allow prints of black and white, bright red and white, or other strong contrasts to dry slowly—they tend to run.

These little tips might keep your clothes looking perfect all year!

Velcro® for Babies' Outfits

For an alternative to grippers or snaps for babies' one-piece pants outfits, purchase a piece of one-inch wide Velcro® the length of the leg and crotch seam.

Cut the strip in half lengthwise, and stitch half of it on one seam and half on the other. It takes only a second to press the strips together. When changing diapers, they're easier to open than snaps or grippers.

Be sure, though, to keep the pants leg closed when machine washing, or the Velcro® will stick to other fabrics.

Reinforce Buttons

To reinforce children's buttons, place a small piece of iron-on fabric that matches the garment underneath each button before you sew. This added insurance has kept many a button intact.

Knit Blanket Binding

To replace frayed bindings on blankets, cut strips of knit fabric to the desired width. If you cut the bindings on the crossgrain, there is no need to turn the edges under. Simply sew with a zigzag stitch and you have an attractive, long-wearing, washable trim.

Invisible Thread

When machine stitching tiny hems on printed fabrics, use invisible thread on the bobbin and the regular-colored thread on the top.

By stitching on the wrong side of the garment on the edge of the hem, the invisible thread never shows from the right side.

Handy Bobbins

Keep a large number of bobbins handy to match threads. When finished with the thread, place the bobbin on top of the spool of thread, run a long fastener for trash bags down through the hole in the bobbin and spool, and twist the ends of the fastener together. You can begin to sew at once without having to fill a bobbin each time.

Easy Zipper

For an easy way to put a zipper in pants or skirts, use a nine-inch nylon or Teflon® zipper instead of the usual seven-inch type.

Apply the zipper in the usual way, but leave the two extra inches extending at the top.

Slip the tab of the zipper down and apply the waistband, sewing right across the zipper. Cut off the excess above the seam.

This will give you a smooth application with no uneven stitching when jogging around the zipper tab.

Easy Needle Threading

Threading a sewing machine needle can get on your nerves when you try and try without success. To save your temper, cut the end of the thread at an angle and simply slide it down the groove of the machine needle. This has worked beautifully on all machine needles.

Pattern Tape

Splicing or mending often-used patterns works well if you use the pink paper tape used for hair setting. This tape doesn't dry out, crack or discolor. Keep a roll in your sewing basket. You will be surprised how often you use it.

Press Crease

Here's how they accurately press the creases in pants, as learned from a couture shop in Rome.

After you have cut the slacks, before any construction, fold each of the four pieces (two fronts and two backs) in half lengthwise, right sides out. Make sure the cut edges are lined up evenly; then press the folded edge to about eight inches from the waistband.

If you prefer the creases in front to be stitched, stitch them at this time. Then continue with the construction according to your pattern instructions.

Anchor Metal Buttons

To keep metal coat buttons with a shank from popping off a coat, take the straight "eye" part of a hook and eye set, and put it through the shank of the button. Simply use it as an anchor for the button. Instead of sewing through the shank, which always cuts the threads, sew each end of the eye to your coat. The button itself will be able to slide on this, which gives the button more freedom and it won't snap off.

Pressing Tip

Find a small plastic bottle with a very small hole in the pointed tip (like the ones that come with home hair coloring kits or permanents) and fill with water. When it comes to pressing seams open, simply run down the seams with the tip of the bottle. Allow some of the water to remain on the open seams. Put a press cloth on top and steam them open. The water gets just where you need it with no water rings or iron spots.

Pins for Nylon Net

When working with nylon net, use corsage pins to hold the net in place. They won't fall out and get lost in your fabric as other pins do.

Perfect Curves

When sewing curves such as pocket flaps, rounded collars and rounded cuffs, it's easier than you think to make perfect curves. Just continue with your straight seam stitching to the cut edge of both sides—as you would if the corners were square or pointed.

With a smaller length stitch, go back about two inches before the corner and stitch over the previous seam until you come close to the corner. Curve your stitching to round the corner and continue stitching until you restitch over your previous stitching an inch or two. You will not only have reinforced rounded corners, but they should be nice and even every time.

Shortening Sleeves

To shorten a child's coat or jacket sleeves, simply take a tuck in the sleeve lining only, letting it pull the outer sleeve up with it to the inside. When it needs lengthening (which seems almost immediately with growing children), simply take out the stitching and allow the hem to fall down again. An added benefit is that the shortened hem won't leave a heavy crease mark to fight with after the garment has been lengthened.

No-Slip Patch Pockets

When attaching patch pockets to shirts, jackets, or whatever, attach bits of fusible interfacing to the corners and to the middle of the sides and bottom, and press lightly in place. It holds the pocket beautifully until stitched.

Plastic Shirt Stays

The best way to make permanent stays for shirt collars is to cut them from the plastic lid of a coffee can. These can be cut with shears to the desired width and length and sewed permanently in place in a pocket on the interfacing.

They withstand heat from the dryer or pressing with an iron and are good for the life of the shirt. They are flexible and keep the collar points neatly in place.

Quick Jacket Lining

Replace a worn jacket lining with a plaid flannel shirt. Place the shirt in the jacket, right side out. With a little sewing at cuffs and around sides and collar, you have a warm jacket. It only takes minutes to accomplish.

Actually, because leather jackets aren't too warm, shirt liners will make them more serviceable than ever before!

Turning Belts

When making narrow strips for trim that have to be turned after stitching, such as belts and bias trimmings, use a new unsharpened pencil with an end eraser. Stitch the strip across one end and insert the pencil, eraser first, and see how easy it is to turn right side out. The eraser pushes very easily and the length of the pencil helps much better than anything else.

Needle Threader

Make a needle threader from a very fine copper wire. Just double it over, and it slips right through the needle. It is much sturdier than the commercial threaders.

Pocket Shaper

When making a patch pocket with rounded ends, cut the shape of the pocket out of lightweight cardboard. Use this to shape the pocket when pressing in the curve and seam allowance. Both pockets will be identical in this way.

Prevent Button Damage

You can prevent damage to buttons while cleaning if you take a small square of foil and wrap it closely around each button. Be sure to squeeze it very tight. It will stay on while the garment is being washed or dry-cleaned.

Signed Quilt

Quilts are precious and should be cherished always. On every quilt you make, receive, or give, embroider the name of the person to receive, the person who made the quilt and the date. Children love to read the bottom corner as they make the beds.

Which Needle Is Which?

To see whether or not you have a straight needle or a ball-point needle in your sewing machine, leave a small scrap of fabric from the last garment you have worked on under the machine foot. You can tell at a glance whether or not you should switch needles when you start to sew again.

Chapter 2
NOT FOR BEGINNERS ONLY

One of the exciting projects you can share with your teenagers is a sewing project. Whether it is a success or a failure depends on your approach. I have seen many teenagers give up in tears because their mothers didn't know how to handle the situation.

First, and most important, let them make the decisions. A few suggestions would be to start with a smock top to wear with jeans, a wrap-apron dress, a sundress that can be worn with T-shirts or without, a wrap skirt that requires hardly any fitting, pants, shorts or swim cover-ups. (See figure 1.)

Fabric selection and pattern are the two most important parts of the project. Choose a fabric that is firm, of good quality and that could be ripped if necessary (certainly avoid the India gauzes for the first project). Preshrink all fabrics for this sewing project.

Get your daughter a sewing basket of her own, complete with her own supplies. By all means, let her use your sewing machine. A good machine can't do anything but improve with use. Do anything that will encourage her to continue to sew anything she wants. She'll improve with experience, and of course, sewing lessons will help anyone.

Teens have a knack for starting projects and never finishing them, but we found a successful solution to that in my family.

When my girls wanted to make something, they selected their own fabric and patterns and paid for them out of their own allowances. When the garment was completed, they were reimbursed in full, so they never ended up paying for their clothes.

This developed good habits, plus it introduced them to the joy of sewing with fine quality fabrics. Today their first love is still making their own clothes.

Right Age for Sewing

Q. I am wondering if you would tell us what is the right age for young girls to begin sewing, and what should they make to keep them from getting discouraged?

A. As to your question about the age when girls could begin to sew, that would depend en-

15

tirely on the desire on the part of the girl. Some of them will start making doll clothes very early and really enjoy creating make-believe clothes. For the most part, I usually recommend eleven or twelve as a good age for any type classes.

First, to get them really excited, let them choose their own fabrics (don't make the mistake of having them start with some fabric you have had lying around for years). You've got to be excited in the beginning or the finest teacher can't make you like to sew.

I would suggest trying to enroll the girls in small classes, preferably those that only last four weeks; then they will have plenty of time for other activities.

A good project to begin with would be the sundress, a wrap skirt or pants with a vest and top. It's best to begin with something very simple until they get the feel of it; then on to more difficult patterns.

You must overlook a few mistakes—don't do anything to dampen their enthusiasm. After all, sewing is work, to a degree, and you have to be happy with the results or the work isn't worth the effort.

Sewing your own clothes is very much "in" today and most girls really love it.

Starting Right

Q. My girls want to take sewing lessons and I want to start them out right. Since clothes are so casual, what could they make that they would actually wear?

A. A few ideas for their first project would be tennis dresses, wrap skirts, shorts, apron dresses, warmup jackets, and any variety of the popular smock tops. There are many other patterns for them to choose from—I only named a few as starters.

Don't let them begin with plaids or anything that has to be matched. If they sail through the first garment, they can choose something more difficult the second time. Praise them. If their desire grows, they'll have a beautiful hobby. I don't know of anything more rewarding.

Tips for Beginners

Q. My daughter wants to learn to sew, but her school doesn't offer a home economics course. Can you give her a few tips?

A. I would send her to a professional sewing class that is designed for girls her age. Often, youngsters will take instruction from an outsider more readily than their parents.

Once your daughter has started sewing and has decided on a particular project, the important thing to remember is that it's going to be HER work. Allow her to choose the pattern and fabric she wants, but remind her that it is best to keep things simple.

It is also important to remember that YOUR attitude toward your daughter's sewing is very important. Often mothers come into my shop, only to tell their daughters, "Don't get anything expensive—you're just going to ruin it." Anything that takes time to learn needs all the encouragement you can give.

Adult Beginner

Q. I'm in my twenties, and would like to learn to sew. What would you suggest?

A. You'll make it. Just remember, everything that is worn has been made by someone, so why not you?

Too many beginners make the mistake of burdening themselves with patterns that require difficult details, lots of fitting, and hard-to-work-on fabrics. This does discourage one. There's nothing like making something and being able to wear it almost immediately. Gradually work difficult patterns as your skills develop.

For starters, try a wrap skirt. Skirts are definitely "in," there is virtually no fitting, and making them is a matter of learning to sew straight seams. You don't even have to insert a zipper.

Don't forget the butcher's apron—you'll see it everywhere young fashion is shown. Again, no fitting, no zipper or other difficult details. Butcher's aprons can be worn with T-shirts, your favorite blouses or as a sundress without a shirt or blouse.

Smock tops, wrap tops or elastic scoop-neck peasant blouses would be another choice.

Select fabric that is relatively easy to work. Select a good quality fabric. You will have to rip a seam here and there. It's a part of sewing, so choose a fabric that can be ripped without falling apart.

Today you will find denims, poplins, butcher linens, and many more fabrics simple to work with.

Search the trim market to give your garments individuality. The first compliment you get will make your spirits soar and you will be well on the way to a new love—home sewing.

Try Sewing

Q. I am so tired of expensive prices and poor quality clothing that I want to try sewing. Some of my friends have offered to help me. What do you recommend?

A. Be sure your friends sew well enough that you want to copy them. I still strongly urge all of you to take some professional lessons whenever possible. The money spent is nothing compared to starting out on the right foot.

Most beginners start with a pattern that is much too difficult for them; this immediately takes the fun out of sewing. Choose a pattern with very few pieces and relatively little fitting because you must learn to stitch a straight seam first.

Choose a good quality, firmly woven fabric. Beginners don't know enough to work on sleazy, cheap fabric. You'll soon learn the value of your time and realize it takes time to work on both kinds of fabric. Make your time worthwhile by working on the best—you'll be glad you did.

Be patient. Don't be in too much of a hurry; learn to do each step right. I'm convinced the most frustrated sewers are only frustrated because they are trying something that they are not educated to do.

Learn to study ready-to-wear and fashion magazines for your ideas. A home sewer often uses too many details and the wrong trims. The most expensive clothes are very simple in line.

Be enthusiastic and always visualize the finished garment. Each step of the way will not bog you down if you're optimistically looking forward to wearing your garment and starting a new one. Good luck.

Beginning Fitting

Q. I am just beginning to sew for myself and my biggest problem is how to fit myself. Do you have any tips?

A. I will give you a few tips, but may I also suggest that you ask a friend who sews to help you get started. Of course, my first recommendation would be to take sewing classes if at all possible. These classes will teach you how to alter your patterns to fit you before you begin cutting out your garments.

Too many women purchase the same size pattern as they wear in ready-to-wear; instead, measure your chest to determine your pattern size. Then, cut the pattern out and stitch it up with no thought to the fitting. You will find that after you have been sewing awhile, the clothes you thought fitted you really didn't fit properly at all.

NEVER fit your garments with the wrong side out. Everyone has some variation in their body, and if you fit your clothes wrong side out, you will be adjusting the opposite side of your body.

I have always suggested machine stitching about three inches down from the underarm to hold the garment together enough to be able to slip it on. Also stitch the shoulders. For the side seams, you may pin-baste them before the fitting.

This means the seams should extend out from the garment. You are placing the two wrong sides of fabric together and pinning with the pins in a vertical position on the seamline. In this way, it isn't too difficult to change the position of these pins should you need to take in the waist and hipline.

After you have completed the fitting (don't fit too tightly to the body), separate the seams and rub chalk on the pins. When you unpin the garment and repin it so you can begin stitching on the wrong side, you will be able to see the pin marks.

NEVER press anything, seams or darts, until you have had a fitting. Today's clothes skim the body and aren't very fitted, so you are lucky to be learning at this time.

Sewing Straight

Q. I am a real beginner at sewing, but even though I'm only eleven years old, I already love it. I have trouble keeping my sewing on a straight line and also keeping it even around curves for my collars and neckline. What do you suggest I do?

A. Years ago when I began teaching young girls (as well as the older ones), I recommended drawing circles, curves, and squares on plain paper and also using lined tablet paper for practice.

Don't thread the sewing machine. Instead, work with the needle only and machine stitch all the straight lines, curves and circles. You will gradually find out how to control the paper to stitch nice rounded curves as well as your straight stitching. This is so important because it will save you lots of time ripping later on. After you become accurate enough to stitch right on the lines, be sure to change the machine needle, which will be dull from stitching on paper.

Straight Seams

Q. It seems that my most difficult detail to master is stitching a straight seam. What should I do?

A. This is one detail that seems to plague most sewers, even if they aren't beginners.

The first thing to do is mark your seam with a tracing wheel or a sharp-edged piece of chalk. If there is any danger of the color showing through your fabric, though, you must be very selective in your marking.

There are other aids to stitching a straight seam. You can buy a magnetic seam guide that is placed on your machine. When not in use, this guide simply pushes out of the way. Also, seam widths are marked on most sewing machine throat plates.

The secret to using the last two devices is to keep your eye on the marking or the magnetic guide to be sure the edge of the seam is touching the marks. Most women have a tendency to watch the needle instead of the cut edge of the fabric, and this makes for uneven stitching.

Sewing Errors

Q. Could you point out what the sewing errors are that scream "homemade"?

A. When these errors appear, the person who did the sewing was unaware of the results. Here are a few of the most obvious details that indicate a garment is homemade.

One of the first dead giveaways is when you see facings creeping out and showing from the right side of the garment. Another giveaway is a collar that curls up like a dog's ear instead of a professional-looking rolled collar.

Choosing fabrics that are not suitable for the pattern and choosing a more difficult pattern than you can cope with are common errors. A seamstress needs to spend more time looking at better ready-to-wear and fashion magazines for ideas. You'll find that very simple designs with beautiful fabrics usually look best. Besides, it's important to use quality fabric for the best results.

Another sewing error is a poorly pressed garment with edges that look lumpy. If you're not an experienced seamstress and you don't understand pressing techniques, rely on a professional tailor or dry cleaner and have your garment pressed when completed.

Sleeves shouldn't pucker. Instead, they should have a beautiful smooth cap.

A noticeable error is a hand-stitched hem on knits with tiny stitches that pull the fabric too tight. In most cases, hems of knits should be machine-stitched about ½ inch from the fold of the hem. Be sure to cut off the excess and never finish the hem of a knit with lace or seam binding.

Hems that are too deep look very homemade. The weight of the fabric is too heavy to avoid an ugly ridge. Hems of coats should be about two inches wide, and skirt hems should be about 1½ inches wide unless they are bias. Bias skirts and knits should have very small hems, no wider than one inch.

Chapter 3
GOOD SEWING MACHINES MAKE HAPPY SEWERS

As you know, there are dozens of sewing machines available, and each one is represented as being the best. It's very difficult to make an honest comparison due to the pressures that are usually placed on the purchaser.

Because a sewing machine is one of the major purchases in any family, it is something you must study carefully and not make snap decisions. I have advised you to check many machines because they all have different features.

You will have to make a few decisions.

Would you like the free-arm feature which makes it much simpler to get to those tight spots such as sleeves, pants, and necklines? A control which lifts the presser foot is another big plus for the gal who will be doing a lot of sewing.

Decide whether you need all the decorative stitches or just the stretch stitches. Most of all, decide just how much you can afford to spend. The cheapest is not always the best buy.

I recommend that you purchase the latest consumer guide which has a complete comparison of all sewing machines. It brings out the good and bad points, most of which you wouldn't discover until after you had made the purchase. The consumer guide is worth every penny because it is an honest report made by professionals in the field.

Whenever you shop for a sewing machine, be sure to be relaxed and allow plenty of time. A sewing machine is expensive, so be sure and select one that will do everything you want it to. Don't let anyone pressure you into a purchase you aren't sure about.

Some shops will let you borrow a sewing machine for a few days so you may try it at home. If this is not possible, try it in the store, and make sure you actually try the machine yourself—don't just watch the salesperson.

The warranty of the machine is one of the most important things to consider when making a purchase. Check it carefully to see exactly what it covers.

While shopping, check the features of the machine. Are the stitches even on both sides of the fabric? Is there speed control for slow as well as fast stitching? Is the machine relatively quiet and free of vibrations? Are the buttonholes easy to make and are they perfect?

Be sure to check the details on tension adjustment. One Swiss-made machine has perfected tension so it never needs adjusting, regardless of fabric. Find out if the machine is easy to thread, and if it is easy to clean and oil.

Also, when you purchase a machine, be sure you receive personal lessons on how to use it. With the proper care and a happy, knowledgeable sewer, a sewing machine will last for years.

Make a Needle Pad

Be good to your sewing machine—it may only be as good as the needle you use. Did you realize that many problems you have in sewing the newer fabrics are the direct result of the needles you are using?

The days of sewing with a machine needle until it breaks are gone forever. Today we change needles with every fabric. We now have special needles for leather, for topstitching, and for knits. They all look similar and are difficult to distinguish one from another, so I have devised a good idea for you. It works for us.

Make yourself a needle pad using any woven fabric, preferably a solid color because you will be marking on it. A five- or six-inch square is adequate. If you use two layers of fabric, you could finish the edges with a decorative machine stitch.

With a marking pen, print the types of needles you will be using, and keep a special marking for different sizes. Instead of putting the needles back into the package they came in, simply pin in the proper place on your needle pad. You'll be amazed how easy it is to change a needle when you know exactly what you are doing.

Use Correct Needle

Many sewers wonder whether to use ball-point needles for everything, why they have stitches that skip, or why threads pull when fabric is stitched.

Definitely do not use ball-point needles for everything—use them for knitted fabrics only. Ball-point needles come in different sizes. If you are working with a tricot knit or a fine matte jersey, it is important that you use the finest or smallest size needle and change sizes according to the weight of the fabric. Many times, skipped stitches you experience in knits occur because of using the wrong size or type of needle.

A blunt needle will cause the threads to pull as you stitch your fabric. Once these threads are pulled, they usually will never be able to be disguised. Use a regular needle for all woven fabrics, again changing the size according to the weight of the fabric.

If you sew over pins, you will have to change needles more often, as the needles tend to get tiny snags on them which could tear fabric. Two new needles available are the needles especially designed for real leather and the needles designed for buttonhole twist.

Your sewing machine is an expensive item to be treasured and taken care of. It's sturdy and yet very delicate, so treat it with "tender loving care" and it will perform lovingly for you.

It's false economy to try to sharpen needles. This is the least expensive accessory you will use, and sharpening is never very successful. Often emery bits that come off the needles from the needle sharpeners can clog up your machine.

While we're on the subject of your machine, here are just a few other reminders. One, do not blow the lint from your machine. Brush it out instead (and often). The moisture from your breath when you blow on this fine mechanism can actually cause corrosion.

Also, be careful when choosing oil to lubricate your machine. Never use household oil; instead, always use only the clear, white oil that is made expressly for sewing machines. Most guarantees on sewing machines will not hold good if you have used the wrong type of oil and it has permanently gummed up the delicate moving parts of your machine.

How to Love Your New Sewing Machine

First of all, anything that is mechanical and new requires extra patience. You must learn the habits of your new love backwards and forwards.

Don't take the easy route and crawl back to your old machine—even once. Read and follow the instruction book. Take any lessons the company has to offer. They are invaluable.

Purchase a complete new set of machine needles, all sizes and types. The wrong needles can also throw delicate tension mechanisms off.

Keep your machine in perfect condition. Learn where to apply oil and be sure to use sewing machine oil.

Lint from synthetics builds up rapidly in the bobbin case. Purchase a small poster paint BRISTLE (not plastic) brush and learn to brush all exposed parts. A soft cloth should be kept handy to wipe other parts.

A new machine takes some breaking in, so use it, and use it, and use it.

Keep the Needle in High Position

Q. One of the most frustrating experiences for me is rethreading my sewing machine needle. It seems to always come unthreaded as I begin to sew. When I take my work out of the machine, it's often difficult to remove. Because of the tightness of the thread, it breaks again. What am I doing wrong?

A. This is a common complaint. It's such a simple thing that is causing your problem you won't believe it. Somewhere you have forgotten one of the basic rules of a sewing machine. Don't remove the part of your garment you have just stitched until you first turn the wheel by hand so the needle is at its highest position.

Your fabric will come out nicely and without breaking the thread because there will be no tension.

When you begin again with the needle in high position, the thread will not shorten or tighten up as you begin stitching. There will be no further problems.

If the needle isn't in the highest position when you end your stitching, just turn the wheel by hand until it is. This will become automatic once you are aware of it.

Skipped Stitches

Q. I have an old machine that belonged to my mother, and it has always behaved beautifully for me. Now I am having problems. My latest was making a heavy latex nylon swimsuit—the machine kept skipping stitches, and yet the repairman tells me that nothing is wrong with my machine. Can you offer any suggestions?

A. All of you must remember that today we have a whole new world of fabrics—the stretchables, sheer knits, and such—many of which were unheard of ten years ago. The old sewing machines simply weren't made for these fabrics of today, and many of them simply won't work because of the tension, feed control, and so on.

In the case of the swimsuit you are making, be sure to use a larger size ball-point needle. The stretch nylon is a tough knit and probably too heavy for your present needle. You will have to experiment to get the best results.

If you are shopping for a new sewing machine, I can't recommend too highly one that has built-in tension that adjusts to the weight of the fabric and thread automatically.

Most important, test a new sewing machine's ability on those difficult fabrics, such as knits of all types and stretch fabrics. Test for ripping as well as stitching because we do have to rip occasionally, and some of the stretch stitches available cannot be ripped.

Sewing Fine Knit

Q. I'm in real trouble. I have a beautiful piece of material that looks like a very fine knit. The tension on my sewing machine is perfect for cottons and woven fabrics, but when I try to sew on this fabric, my machine skips stitches. What can I do?

A. These fine knits that resemble matte jersey do present a problem to many of you with older sewing machines. They simply weren't made to handle this knit of fabric.

I find there is no definite answer. You will have to play around with your own sewing machine and try to find the solution. I will tell you about a few tips you might check into.

First, are you using a ball-point needle? For a fine knit, you must use a fine needle—a number 9 or 11 is best. Often it is necessary to lower the presser foot so that it is closer to the throat plate of your machine, which would cause less slippage of your fabric.

If your throat plate has the long slot in it, the one you use for the zigzag stitch, change it to the one that only has the single hole in it for the needle when straight stitching. This again eliminates extra play for the fabric. You also might try the regular stitching foot instead of the one used for zigzag stitching.

If you have tried all of these things, you may have to change the tension. I am ordinarily opposed to this because once you fiddle with the tension, it usually takes a professional sewing machine repairman to get it straightened out again.

For any of you who are contemplating purchasing a new machine, insist that the demonstrator use these hard-to-sew knits to check the machine stitching. Any machine can sew on muslin, but it takes precision workmanship to handle today's fabrics.

Puckered Seams

Q. I am in tears over a jersey dress I am making. I've done everything you have suggested—a ball-point needle, polyester thread—and still my seams pucker. Have you any suggestions?

A. It is so difficult to answer this question without actually seeing the fabric. However, there are still several areas to be checked. Be sure you aren't stitching with too small a stitch. I recommend ten to twelve stitches per inch. Some sewing machines will simply not stitch on these knits, although with careful adjustments, most of them can be constructed with just about any machine. It's always best to make a sample stitching on a scrap of fabric before proceeding with your garment.

Sewing Machine Gift

Q. I have been sewing on a sewing machine I inherited from my mother. Now I'm doing so much more sewing than before and would really like a new machine. My problem is that my

Fig. 2 — Sewing Machine Gift

husband is planning to surprise me and I'm sure he'll purchase the wrong brand. I have my heart set on the one I would love to own. How can I point him in the right direction?

A. I can't tell you how often I have had this question come up and how important it is to let your husband know that it's like you purchasing some tools for him without the knowledge you need.

If you have already selected the machine you want, let him know. If not, ask him to please let you make your own selection when you have plenty of time to look them over. A sewing machine can be your best friend for many, many years if it does what you want it to do. (See figure 2.)

Chapter 4
FABRICS

About Wool

There are many types of wool, some as smooth as silk and others that are very wiry and suitable for coats only. We also have many wool blends.

Since wool is a living fiber, it doesn't require cleaning as often as the miracle fibers of today. I usually suggest you depend on a reputable dry cleaner to keep your better woolens looking perfect.

Yes, there are washable wools, too. Be sure to check the fiber content and the washability when you make your purchase. Perhaps you would want to wash slacks, skirts, and shirt jackets that haven't been tailored like jackets and coats. Again, I recommend prewashing before construction.

Many of you have asked if wool needs to be preshrunk before construction if you are going to have your garment dry-cleaned. In most cases, no. Better wools that are available for the home sewer are ready for the needle.

If you purchase wools from a foreign country when you are on a trip, or if a friend should bring you some, play safe and either preshrink it yourself or take it to a dry cleaner and have them preshrink it.

Skirts and pants made of wool are seldom underlined. Instead, if you don't want the wool close to your body, you may apply a separate lining to skirts, hemming each separately. Also apply a separate lining to pants, catching it to the waistband, zipper and hemming it loosely to the hem of the pants, allowing at least ½ inch ease to avoid pulling.

Interfacing for wool coats and jackets should have some hair in the interfacing to keep the fronts from becoming too stiff and allowing the lapels and collar to roll nicely. One I like is called Acro by Armo Company.

Press seams with your steam iron. Faced edges must be pressed carefully with a chemically treated press cloth.

A beautiful wool garment should be tailored to perfection. This would be an excellent project for fall, and if possible, take a good course in custom tailoring to help you over the techniques of which you are unsure. You must never have that loving-hands-at-home look to a tailored garment.

Sewing with Corduroy

Q. I want to sew with corduroy. Would you give me some tips?

A. You must remember that corduroy is a pile fabric; therefore, it has a nap, which means that all pieces of the pattern must be placed in the same direction. This often requires extra fabric. To get the rich luster of corduroy, cut with the smooth pile running up. If you cut with the pile running down, the fabric will look lighter and shinier.

To determine which way the pile runs, lay the fabric on a table and stroke it lightly along the length. A smooth feeling means you are going with the pile; a rough feeling means you are going against it.

Carefully watch the lengthwise grain since there are ridges which must be vertical. For interesting details, corduroy could be cut crosswise for an Ottoman effect. It may also be cut on the bias. Try interesting variations.

Use a slightly longer machine stitch for any pile fabric. It may also be necessary to loosen the pressure on the presser foot of your machine. If you pin-baste, place the pins at right angles to the seams and pin within the seam allowance only (pins will crush your fabric if you stitch over them). Finish seams with an overcast stitch by hand or machine.

Buttonholes, if made on the sewing machine, must be stitched very close together (just enough room to slit the center) to avoid ragged edges when cut. If you prefer bound buttonholes, make your strips on the bias.

For smooth, professional-looking hems and facings, overcast the edges by machine. Then stitch ¼ inch from the edge. Unless the hems are to be machine-stitched near the raw edge for a tailored look, just roll back the raw edges about ¼ inch, catch the needle in the underside of the hem and pick up one or two threads of the skirt, keeping all your stitches very loose.

Pressing corduroy is no problem if you don't overdo it. Your iron should never touch the right side of the fabric. Press the fabric face down on a thickly padded table or board (terry cloth is best for the padding). Then place the steam iron very gently on the area to be pressed, lift and continue to move iron gently. Never press hard like you do with ordinary ironing. Professional dry cleaners also do a remarkable job with finish pressing.

Corduroys are fun, easy to sew with, and beautiful. But, you must take a few precautions for success.

Corduroy on Cross-Grain

Q. I recently saw a picture of several corduroy suits that had the rib effect running horizontally instead of vertically. Is this look something new? Do we have to have a special pattern for it?

A. You are very observant. All designers try new tricks with old favorite fabrics. I have seen several garments made with the corduroy cut on the cross grain and I found them most attractive.

You can use your regular pattern, but instead of using the lengthwise grainline as a guide, you will cut the garment on the cross-grain. It would still be very important to begin all the pieces of your pattern at the same selvage edge so they're all cut in the same direction.

Proceed to complete your garment just as if it would have been cut on the vertical.

Corduroy Skirt

Q. I love wrap skirt patterns but hesitate to use them for corduroy because of the direction of the ribs. Have you tried a circular skirt on this type of fabric?

A. Yes, and I loved it. The center front has the ribs of corduroy running horizontally because the skirt is cut on the cross-grain, but the direction changes as the circle changes. Since there are no seams, the shadings are most attractive.

Once again, we're shown how versatile fabrics can be.

Acrylic

Q. Does acrylic stretch? I would like to make a pantsuit in the woolish look in acrylic and am wondering about the seat area of the pants and the knees.

A. The knit fabric you are referring to won't stretch just because it is acrylic any more than any other knit would stretch. It all depends on the quality of your knit fabric.

Before making any purchase of knit fabric, give it a good hard stretch and check the immediate recovery. If the fabric stays limp and slightly stretched out of shape, it should not be used for a tailored garment. Instead, it should be used for the soft drapable dress that doesn't have areas fitted so tight they could bulge out of shape.

Qiana®

Q. Please clear up an argument I am having with a friend of mine. She tells me that Qiana® is a polyester and the clerk in the fabric shop didn't seem to know. What exactly is it?

A. Qiana® is 100 percent nylon, and the name is a trademark used exclusively by DuPont. Originally, Qiana® was out of reach for the average woman. It was so expensive that it was used by the designers only. Today, with more availability, it is very reasonably priced and comes in many weights and types, including velvet, taffetas, silk-type twills, and knits.

Everyone who uses this fabric seems to fall in love with it. It is very luxurious, so why not try it?

Qiana® is completely washable and requires no pressing. It is great for travel and packing, and is a year-round fabric. If you live in a very hot climate, you may find it a bit warm to wear since it is nylon.

Qiana® Shirtwaist

Q. I'm making a shirtwaist dress out of satin Qiana® knit. It is rather revealing and I would like to try to make it double, at least in the bodice, but I can't figure out how to go about this. Can you help me?

A. If the Qiana® knit isn't too lightweight, you may decide to only make the bodice front double, although both front and back can be done very well.

As for the front bodice, since it is a shirtwaist with a button closing, you must place the foldline of the front (which is ⅝ inch beyond the center front) on the fold of your fabric. Instead of cutting the regular facing extension, your extension will go back to the side seam.

Your construction will be the same. Just baste the two layers of fabric together at the neck edges, shoulders, underarms, and lower edge of the bodice. Then you proceed the same as if it were just one layer of fabric.

If you have cut the facing extension by error, just make a seam at the edge of the facing and extend the facing to the side seams. This is very popular with very expensive clothes, and it's a nice couturier touch to add to your own dressy clothes. Please don't consider making the bodice double unless the fabric is very lightweight.

Fig. 3 – Print from India

Print from India

Q. A friend of mine bought me a lovely printed piece of fabric from India. My problem is that I have noticed the print is irregular—it overlaps at times and doesn't seem as perfect as the prints that are made in this country. Am I being superconscious of imperfections? I feel if I make it up, I will constantly have to make excuses for it. It actually looks like a second. What should I do?

A. Use the print and enjoy it. The imperfections you speak about are a sign that the fabric was printed by hand. This is done with blocks dipped in color, and often they do overlap slightly. Only machines create perfect prints.

Sometimes a slight imperfection is a sign of value. There is not enough creativity available, and of the few things that can be boasted as handmade, the India fabrics are one of them. (See figure 3.)

India Gauze

Q. I am just beginning to sew and want to make a smock top out of India gauze. Can you tell me what kind of interfacing to use so it won't be too stiff?

A. If you notice, most of the shirts and tops made of India gauze fabric have very little construction. I would suggest choosing a pattern that has very little stiffening.

For a very light interfacing, try a very lightweight underlining. For collars and cuffs of a more tailored design, use featherweight all-bias Pellon®.

Most important, be sure to preshrink any India fabric. It is made of cotton that has never been preshrunk, so you must allow extra yardage. Also, misprints or imperfections in the fabric are all part of the natural look. These fabrics come from individual families in India and no two are alike. Imperfections are a sign the work was done by hand, so please do not expect it to be of the quality you find in domestic and other imported fabrics.

Silk Linen

Q. I just finished a beautiful pair of slacks out of pure silk linen. I lined the slacks and they fit perfectly. After I had them dry-cleaned, they were too short. How could I have avoided this problem? Should the fabric have been preshrunk?

A. Usually a fabric that will be dry-cleaned doesn't need to be preshrunk, although there is a possibility that your cleaners are using too much moisture. Always be sure that your materials have been preshrunk. When you are using washable fabrics, you must always preshrink them in the same temperature you will be using when you are actually wearing and washing the garment.

I would suggest that you do the following to avoid disappointment.

Instead of finishing the hems of the pants perfectly, finish them for the first time with long, loose stitches. When you wash or send your garment out to be cleaned for the first time, remove the stitches from the hem; then remark them after cleaning and hem them again. This extra few minutes could save you countless disappointments later.

You might also consider doing this with ready-made pants. They, too, have been known to shrink considerably when being washed or dry-cleaned.

Pure Silk

Q. With the return of pure silk in designer clothes, could you tell me where this beautiful fabric can be purchased and offer some details about how to work with it?

A. Silk has been coming back into favor for the past few years. In fact, there is a big return to all the pure fibers, wool and cotton, as well as silk.

There are many better fabric resources that now carry quite a selection of pure silk. Perhaps you will have to inquire at a larger city, hopefully not too far from where you live.

Silk is one of the most luxurious of all fibers. It is warm in the winter and cool in the summer (quite the opposite from synthetics). It is a year-round fabric. Therefore, you will find yourself getting a lot of wear from a silk garment.

First, check the width of the fabric. Silk is often woven on a loom that is only thirty-six or forty inches wide; however, the new American silks are usually forty-five inches wide.

Be sure to get new pins for any project in silk. Get very fine pins (usually labeled silk pins). NEVER use a ball-point pin. You must also use a very fine sewing machine needle, usually a number 9 or 11, not ball-point.

Never mark the fabric with a wax chalk. The wax will show through when the garment is pressed. Check the machine stitching on a sample of your fabric before you begin. If the seam puckers, check the tension. Don't depend on pressing to remove the puckers.

If your sewing machine has two throat plates, one for regular stitching and one with the wider opening for zigzag stitching, by all means use the throat plate with the single small opening. The wider opening causes too much play in the fabric and could cause it to pucker. For some sheer silks, it may be necessary to use a layer of tissue paper between the throat plate and the fabric to prevent puckering.

Watch the tension setting on your sewing machine to be sure the setting is correct. If the tension is too tight, puckering could occur. To correct this, loosen the bobbin tension slightly. Always be sure to check on a fabric sample before you work on your garment.

Ten to twelve stitches per inch would be correct. Lightly pull the fabric as it feeds through the machine to reduce puckers. All seams should be finished to avoid raveling. I prefer hand overcasting. It only takes minutes, and there is less chance of drawing up the thread too tight. Cut edges could also be turned over and stitched close to the edge.

Linings and underlinings: Sheer silks such as broadcloth or crepe de chine are very seldom lined. Their beauty is dependent on their whisper weight. Silk shantung, linen or twill silk are usually underlined or lined to retain the shape of the crisp tailoring. Skirts and pants are more satisfactory if underlined to prevent any chance of pulling the seams.

Remember that buttons, zippers or whatever is to be used for closings must be very lightweight to prevent distortion of the garment. Of course, when you have underlined the garment, this is no problem. Zippers should be applied by hand (on both sides of the zipper).

Dry cleaning is usually recommended; however, it is not a must. Some silk garments may be successfully handwashed in mild suds and line-dried. Never machine-wash silk or dry it in the electric dryer.

The real joy of sewing is learning to sew with these luxury fabrics. I hope some of you will begin with silk this spring, even if you only make a scarf or blouse for a start.

If you wonder why ready-made garments of silk are so prohibitive in price, it's because of the cost of the fabric plus the skill it takes to construct. With careful handling, you can create your own costume room garment.

Proper Needle

Q. I finally got the courage to make a shirt of pure silk. My biggest problem seemed to come from machine stitching. Wherever I have stitched a seam, the threads of the silk seem to be pulled. Should I have used tissue paper?

A. Tissue paper is often used under pure silk chiffon because it slips so easily, and stitching through the paper keeps the seams more stable. Your problem is a simple one to answer and one I hope everyone will remember.

When sewing silk, you must use a very fine needle, not a ball-point, and be sure the needle has never been used. Once a needle is used, especially with polyesters or any synthetics that dull a needle, it will pierce the threads of your fabric and cause them to look pulled (there is no way you can erase this look).

I can't stress too often or too much the importance of the proper machine needle. Many women feel the only time to change to a new needle is when the original needle breaks. I think you should use a new sewing machine needle with every new garment you make. It is the cheapest way to guarantee a beautiful stitch with no pulls.

When you replace a needle, be sure to destroy the one you have removed. If you save it, you will use it again at the wrong time. Incidentally, when replacing the needle, be sure you get the new needle all the way up the slot and in the proper position. The curved side of the top of the needle should be placed according to the direction you will be threading your needle.

Some machines are threaded from left to right, others from right to left, and still others from front to back. The position of the needle is very important for perfect stitching.

Sewing with Silks

Q. While in Hong Kong and Thailand, I couldn't resist buying some silk cloth. Now, however, I'm not sure how the cloth should be treated. Because it is so beautiful, I will probably have it dry-cleaned. I was wondering, though, if I should wash it before making garments out of it?

A. Although pure silk can be washed, some types of cloth look nicer if they are dry-cleaned. One thing should be stressed, though—if you are intending to wash the garment after it is made, be sure to prewash the fabric. If the garment is to be dry-cleaned, this is not necessary.

Also, if you intend to wash the garment, all the linings and interfacings must also be washable.

I suggest that when sewing, you use one of the finer, imported, 100 percent long staple polyester threads such as Metrosene. Pure silk thread is almost impossible to find.

I also recommend that you hand-overcast your seams, as thread tends to pull if it is over-cast too tightly by machine. This is done with a loose thread. Be sure to use new machine needles when stitching, preferably a size 11.

I am happy to see silks coming back into fashion, as they are so beautiful, cool and luxurious to wear, and never seem to wear out. Truly, anyone who sews should definitely consider silk in their wardrobe.

Fabric Creases

Q. Last year while in Istanbul, Turkey, I bought a number of meters of fabric that look like silk, but perhaps are a blend of fibers. I had it made into a caftan by a dressmaker, and we found to our horror that the diagonal creases could not be removed. We tried everything, and I am turning to you for help. Naturally I am upset because I will not be able to wear it. Do you have any suggestions?

A. The permanent wrinkles or creases you are referring to often cannot be removed. They are sometimes caused when the fabric is folded onto boards after it has been finished.

Some of the synthetics are heat-treated for permanent finishes, and if they are creased after this process, it is a hopeless case. If you've tried steam, water, and other remedies, try a local dry cleaner. This is the only help I can give you.

This should be a lesson for all of us. When purchasing fabrics, check the type of folds or creases you find in them. If the fabric is only creased at the end of the roll and is machine washable, you have no problems.

To prevent a lot of disappointment, be sure to check this first before making the garment, not after. Fabric should be in perfect condition before beginning to cut and construct.

Fake Fur Coat

Q. I purchased some fake fur fabric for a coat and want to make it up, but I find it difficult to find a suitable pattern. What would you recommend?

A. Actually, almost any pattern for a coat can be used for fake fur as well as wool. I would suggest you shop around and try on some fur coats to see what style is flattering for you; then find a similar pattern.

Usually, fur coats are made a little roomier than cloth coats, so I would avoid any style that seems skimpy. I would also avoid any pattern that had too much detail. The lines should be simple, well cut, and without intricate seaming and design.

Since a fur coat (real or fake) is to be worn over all your clothes, avoid sleeves that are too tight. When doing your construction, try to eliminate a seam on the front edges. Instead, cut the facing as an extension of the front so it can be turned back. Usually double-breasted coats are more suitable. They stay lapped better and are much more comfortable to wear when the weather is cold.

If you live in a climate where it doesn't get cold, settle for one of the casual jackets or collarless coats that can be worn over the shoulders as a lightweight wrap rather than a body-fitting coat.

Fake furs are easy to sew and they need very little, if any, inner construction. After the seams have been stitched, don't press them—just catch-stitch each side of the seam to the inside of the coat.

If the hairs of the fur are caught in the seams, pull them out with a needle from the right side. Often it is advisable to pad the collar with quilting fleece so that it has more of the appearance of a real fur.

Don't put off this coat any longer—you'll probably find it is the easiest garment you've ever made. As one of my customers said, if you make a mistake, just piece the fur and start over again. A real fur coat has many pieces of fur sewn together to form one large piece.

Coating Fabric Nap

Q. I recently bought some very expensive coating fabric that has a long-haired nap effect. However, I'm not sure about the direction it should be cut. What is your opinion?

A. Coatings that have the addition of fur fiber, or any texture that gives a napped look, should be cut with the nap running down. In other words, think about petting a beautiful animal—you want to smooth your garment from the top down, just like you would smooth the fur down on an animal. Since the hair is usually long, it would be most unattractive to cut the nap in the opposite direction.

In my opinion, this would also apply to the nap of cashmere, camel hair or any combination or blends of these fibers. Most important, though, is to be sure to cut all pieces of your pattern in the same direction.

Chintz

Q. I have seen all kinds of garments that look like they have been made of drapery-type chintz. Can we use this decorator fabric for our clothes, or is there some special place to purchase these chintzes?

A. Today, you will see fabrics intended for home decorating used for ready-to-wear, and dress fabrics used in home decorating. Fabrics must appeal to you because of their value and not as a specific area of use.

The chintz you mentioned has been used for years for rain coats and jackets. They are usually cotton and very comfortable in warmer climates. I can see them combined with solids and used for every kind of garment imaginable.

Just watch one detail when making a selection of chintz—they are usually more crisp and slightly firmer than most garment fabrics. Therefore, you would not use them where there is a need for a soft, very full or gathered look.

One of the most attractive garments I have seen in a long time was a long, reversible oriental jacket that was quilted with chintz on one side. Combined with an oriental blouse-top of chintz and worn over pants, it was stunning.

Border Knits

Q. I have seen so many border knits that are so attractive. However, if we want to copy them, we will have to cut the knit on the cross-grain. How will this hold up, and would you recommend it?

Fig. 4 — Border Knit

A. There are exceptions to every rule; in this case, the design makes the exception. I think you will also find that the type of knit for these border prints is more stabilized than any other type. There is practically no give in either direction, so they would not pull out of shape.

I think everyone should play with these lovely bordered fabrics. They can be so attractive as well as a real challenge. You can use your borders for the sleeves, the hemline, the yokes and collars. (See figure 4.)

Also, they can be cut with the border running lengthwise for bands of trim on shirt dresses. It all depends on the border.

Working with Satin

Q. I would like to make a dressy outfit out of satin—perhaps a new jump suit or pajama pants with a shirt top. Is satin difficult to work with?

A. Satin is not difficult to work with. However, there are a few little techniques that apply only to this fabric. First, don't sew over pins—the pin marks might show.

Synthetic satins aren't as delicate as the silk satins we formerly had. Pressing should be done carefully. Don't use a hot iron. Press rather lightly. Satins shouldn't look ironed. They should almost look unpressed.

Baste your garment for fitting; then stitch your seams. Once they have been stitched, they are difficult to remove if they have to be changed. The needle marks will show. Satin is a very luscious fabric. It is used for daytime as well as evening wear.

By all means, consider making something from this fabric. As with any fabric you are unfamiliar with, take some scraps and test the stitching and pressing before proceeding with your garment. It can save lots of mistakes.

Lightweight Wovens

Q. I'd like to make a pantsuit that looks like wool; however, we live in a climate that is too warm for wool. What would you suggest?

A. I have found some beautiful lightweight woven fabrics that would tailor beautifully. They look and feel like a fabulous lightweight wool and yet they are 100 percent polyester. Others are a combination of polyester and wool or polyester and silk, cotton or linen.

Then we have 100 percent cotton that also looks like wool, plus linen, Italian silk, fibranne (a rayon that looks like linen) and many other combinations.

These are all woven fabrics and you will find a crisper, sharper look if you consider these new elegant fabrics. Most of them are less than $10 a yard and they are usually the same width as wool, which makes them very inexpensive to make.

If you live in a warmer climate, you still need this type of fabric for some of your garments due to air conditioning, which makes the temperature more constant.

You may combine your garment with a very lightweight cotton shirt. Cotton is back in great variety, usually with a combination of polyester which keeps it carefree.

You will also find some lovely 100 percent cotton suitings as well as dress weights that are all treated for wrinkle resistancy.

Please be adventurous and try some new fabrics. They could open up a new world of individuality and excitement for you.

The Linen Look

Q. I have seen some expensive sportswear made of 100 percent linen. I can't believe it. The linen I remember would wrinkle just by looking at it cross-eyed. Is linen really back in style?

A. Yes, linen is very much in today's fashion picture. The expensive 100 percent linen you are referring to is now crease resistant—it has been treated with a finish that resists ordinary creases and wrinkles.

There are also many linen-type fabrics on the market. Most of these are fibranne, which is a linen weave made from rayon fibers. This is almost impossible to crease and yet has the appearance of linen.

There is really nothing lovelier than linen—it tailors so beautifully. You will find it used for blazers, skirts, pants, and many dresses. It lends itself to any pattern that requires a crisp, tailored look. It is super fabric for topstitching or handpicking.

One hundred percent linen is washable. However, when you have a tailored jacket, I think it deserves to be dry-cleaned professionally. You will find it keeps its shape and will have a finish from the professional pressing that Is hard to duplicate when you wash the garment yourself.

If you insist on washing your garment, I wouldn't recommend using linen for the outfit; use a polyester blend or rayon blend fabric instead.

Knit Differences

Q. Please explain the difference between the interlock knits and the matte jersey knits. Which are the easiest to wear and which are the easiest to make?

A. Most matte jerseys are fairly sheer since they are a single knit. Because matte jersey or Qiana® jersey is a single knit, it is inclined to be more stretchable. This requires a little more skill to construct.

Another point to consider with the single knits is that they are very figure-revealing. If your body has any excess bulges, avoid this type of fabric because every line will show. If you use a single knit and don't want a clingy garment, choose a pattern with a shirtwaist look or a fairly loose bodice with a full skirt.

An interlock knit is made with a different construction so that it almost resembles a woven piece of fabric. It is much less stretchy and clingy. It is not nearly as figure-revealing. It is much easier to work with because it has a stable character.

When you purchase an interlock knit, pull the cut edge slightly. You will find it will start to run. The edge that runs should always be the hem of the garment. Don't be alarmed. After the hem has been stitched, it won't run any further.

A last work of caution—always cut all knits, either matte jersey or single knit, any double knit, and any interlock knit, in the same direction. This is very important in the appearance as well as the construction of knits.

Knits Will Grow

Q. I just finished one of those long, slinky knit gowns. Before hemming it, I let it hang overnight. The next day it was inches longer than the night before. My friend marked the hem for me and I completed the dress. The next week when I was ready to wear it, it had grown another four inches. What am I doing wrong?

A. Unfortunately, there are many fabrics on the market today that the average home sewer is unaware of, and each requires its own rules.

In the past, I have recommended that any skirt of woven fabric which is cut on the bias hang at least overnight so it will have a chance to relax and hang out. Then the hem is taken and usually will remain fairly even. However, some fabrics will still continue to grow, and you will periodically have to rehem the dress.

In your case, the slinky knit was the reason for your gown to grow right in front of your eyes. This will probably continue. The dress will become longer and narrower as it pulls out of shape.

If your dress is a loosely woven slinky knit, whether it's a panne velvet or jersey, you will not be able to hang it on a hanger as you do your other dresses. If the gown has a waistline seam, fold it over at the waist and hang it up.

If it is cut in one piece, the only solution is to clear out a large drawer and lay it in the drawer, folded over once. Since these knits rarely show a wrinkle, you can shake it out and hang it up for a few minutes. It will look wearable again.

Stretch Knits Only

Q. When a pattern calls for "stretch knits only," what makes this different from one that says "suitable for stretchable fabrics?"

A. When a pattern calls for stretch unbonded knits only, it means the pattern has no fitting darts and the fabric itself will give enough to conform to any shape of your body. If you don't want a garment to cling to every part of your body and reveal every curve, then select another pattern.

If you love knits but don't want the clingy type because of your figure, then you must select a pattern that is marked "suitable for knits". This pattern will usually have bustline shaping or curved seams to take care of your figure. It will not fit your body as closely, but will have more of the appearance of a woven piece of fabric.

If you have a beautiful body and want to show it off, then you will be happy with clingy patterns. The choice is yours.

Price Differences

Q. Can two pieces of fabric that look the same be different? I am referring to some shiny, smooth, satin-type knit fabric that I have found in two different shops. One from our department store was priced two dollars less than fabric that looks the same from our fabric shop. Do fabric shops charge more for their fabric than department stores?

A. Most retailers maintain the same markup on fabric, regardless of whether the shop is a department store, chain fabric shop, or fabric shop.

I think I am aware of the fabric you are referring to. It is a satin Qiana® knit, used quite often in ready-to-wear and fortunately available to the home sewer. This fabric comes in different weights, and this explains the difference in cost.

Often a fabric shop featuring better fabrics will choose the heavier weight for their customers. They may carry some colors in one weight and other colors in the other weight so you will have a choice.

Be sure you examine the name of the fabric and the quality before you think you are overcharged.

Rib Knits

Q. I have just spent a lot of time and effort, to say nothing of money, on a three-piece ensemble of a rib knit fabric. It simply won't keep its shape anywhere. I did use a pattern that called for "stretch knits only." What could possibly be my problem?

A. In the future, you will have to be more careful when selecting your fabric. Rib knits have one failing: Many of them are so loosely woven that the recovery of the stretch factor just isn't up to standards.

When you are purchasing these rib knits, be sure to do your own testing. Check the horizontal stretch and be sure it springs back into shape immediately without leaving a bulge in the fabric. If the fabric is too loosely woven or the fiber doesn't have the proper stretch, no matter what you make, you will be disappointed.

You, as a home sewer, will have to do more research on your fabrics than you ever did before or you will learn the performance isn't what you hoped it would be. Today, we have a whole new world of fabrics and a whole new set of problems. You must learn to rely on the salesperson who really knows to be sure your fabric is compatible with the pattern.

Tubular Knits

When you purchase tubular knits not cut by the manufacturer, be sure to examine the folds to see if the creases have been heatset.

If you find that the creases cannot be pressed out, refold the knit so that none of the pieces of your pattern will be cut on the fold with the crease.

Many times the original crease will disappear when the fabric has been preshrunk.

Keep Terry Knits from Shrinking

Q. I bought some terry cloth to make a long cover-up to wear over my swim suit. I preshrank it. However, when I took it out of the dryer, it was all curled up at both ends and also stretched out of shape. I had a terrible time cutting it out and had to make it shorter than I intended because I lost about six inches due to shrinkage. How could I have avoided this problem?

A. I have often suggested in the past that when shrinking any knits, it's advisable to baste the ends together as well as the sides. This doesn't take long and does help retain the shape of the fabric.

Since terry cloth is a knit, this would have been a good idea for you also. If the terry comes in a tube, then you would only baste the ends together.

To prevent further stretching at neck edges, try using a piece of featherweight, all-bias Pellon® as an interfacing; then topstitch the edges about ¼ inch from the neckline, sleeves, hem or whatever. Terry cloth does stretch easily, so it takes a little extra care during construction.

For slacks and shorts, I would suggest elastic at the waist instead of zippers. Elastic is perfect for long sleeves also. Keep the construction as simple as possible for best results.

Sequin Fabric

Q. I bought some sequin material for a skirt, and now I'm wondering just how to sew this material. Should I bind the seams, and can the sequins be sewn over with my sewing machine?

A. Most of the better quality sequin fabrics have been made with each sequin sewn on with a separate stitch. Because of this, they will not ravel out if you cut your seams or stitch through them.

Yes, you may stitch through the sequins. However, you must not try to press them unless you have done some careful testing, as they will melt with a hot iron. Instead of pressing, achieve the flat, smooth seam appearance by catchstitching each seam open and lightly catching the threads to the garment itself. If you are careful, your stitches will not distort the seams and will not show.

If you are not underlining your fabric for the sheer, see-through look, there is another finish. After stitching your seam, stitch again about ⅛ inch from the first stitching. Cut the seam allowance close to the second stitching and carefully hand-overcast the raw edges.

If you are certain the tension on your sewing machine will not pull the seam too tight, you may overcast these raw edges by machine to avoid further raveling.

Fibranne

Q. I was intrigued with a large picture of a suit with a vest, priced more than $200, in a fashion ad. The fabric mentioned was fibranne. (See figure 5.) No one in the town where I come from knows what fibranne is, and our local fabric store doesn't carry it. Can you please tell us what this is and why it is so expensive?

A. Fibranne is a perfectly wonderful fabric from Italy that first appeared on the market several years ago. Today it is also made by the same company that makes most of the domestic linen in the domestic market.

Fibranne is a rayon fabric with a tight, twisted yarn that defies wrinkling. It is perfect for suits of all types that are to be packed or worn often. It is a cool fabric with a linen-type texture.

It comes in many weights and prices, from around $6 to $12 per yard, depending on the resource and the width of the fabric.

This fabric tailors beautifully. Because of the twisted yarns that prevent wrinkling and give it the crisp factor, it also ravels. I would suggest a little wider seam allowance, and by all means, overcast all the cut edges. It only takes minutes and is well worth the extra time. I would also suggest machine buttonholes since bound buttonholes could ravel out.

Fig. 5 – Fibranne Vest and Skirt

Designer clothes often are priced at several hundred dollars, but you can make yours at a fraction of this cost with the same results. Yet, it is washable; however, I don't recommend washing fibranne because it seems to become a little less crisp. Actually, because of the finish, it doesn't soil easily. What more can I say except that I love it and hope each of you will make something this spring from this marvelous fabric.

Key West Fabric

Q. I am the lucky recipient of four different pieces of Key West fabric. It seems that all of the patterns today are geared for knits; therefore, I am having difficulty in selecting a pattern. Also, should this fabric be underlined and will it shrink when washed?

A. This lovely fabric must never be used for patterns that are marked "for knits only" because the stretch of the knit controls the fitting. You will need darts or gores for the fitting of your fabric. Patterns suitable for woven fabrics will not fit quite as close to your body. They can have some ease and fullness, depending on your figure.

Most of the ready-made garments out of the Key West fabrics are cut rather loose, and darts are used for any fitting. These fabrics work beautifully in sheath dresses, shirt dresses or gored skirts. The fabric is so beautiful that it is not necessary to have lots of details in the pattern. A heavy-type cotton Venice lace is often used for a contrast detail. This lace must also be preshrunk before application.

Most of your designer-type clothes are underlined, but this is no hard and fast rule—it depends on the pattern.

Did you know that this fabric is also used for pants, long skirts and children's clothes, as well as men's shirts and pants? It washes beautifully and is fresh and colorful. It is one of my favorite summer fabrics.

Sewing with Panne Velvet

Q. I recently saw some beautiful velvet cloth I would like to use to make a dinner dress. However, the cloth has a sheen and is knitted, and I don't know how to handle it. Can you help?

A. The type of velvet you are referring to is called panne velvet. Since this fabric is a knit, you must choose your pattern carefully. Select one that says "suitable for knits" or "for knits only."

Panne velvet can be carefully hand washed or dry-cleaned, so choose a pattern with very few seams and details. Never underline this fabric, as it would lose its drapability and cause the seams to pucker.

A fine ball-point needle is used for machine stitching panne velvet. However, before you cut the cloth, check the direction of its nap. Unlike corduroys, velvets and velveteens that ordinarily have the nap going up, I prefer the nap of panne velvet to go down. In other words, I like the fabric smooth to the touch when I run my hand from the shoulder to the hem. Experiment with the length of the stitch on your scraps. Be sure to keep the fabric taut as it feeds through the machine by holding your hand firmly in front and back of the needle as you stitch.

Your seams will often have a tendency to curl inward. To avoid this, press the seams together and use an overlock stitch through both layers of fabric. This should be done in the seam allowance before cutting off the excess.

Try to machine stitch long seams in the direction of the nap. Never try to topstitch this fabric. Hems can be blind-stitched loosely by hand or with your machine. Don't, however, use hem tape or lace on the edge of the hem, as it would restrict the knit.

It is probably best to have your dry cleaner press your garment after it has been completed. However, if you need to press any part of it, always press on the wrong side of the fabric.

Place a piece of the panne velvet on your board so that when you are pressing, you have the two layers of velvet touching each other on their nap sides.

Imitation Suede

Q. I have noticed that men's imitation suede sports jackets are made with conventional seaming and are marked "dry clean only." I wanted to make my husband a leisure jacket and counted on being able to wash it. Why the difference?

A. I checked into this and found that the sports jackets of imitation suede do say "dry clean only" and have conventional methods of construction. I was told that the interfacings, shoulder pads and lining often cannot be washed. Hence, the cleaning instructions.

However, I did find some designer sportswear for men in the form of leisure jackets, and the seaming was of the flat method used in leathers. Since they didn't have the heavy construction details, they could be washed.

Hem in Imitation Suede

Q. I recently bought a dress made of imitation suede. It has two rows of stitching at the hem. The dress is too long and I have to shorten it, but don't know how to sew. Can the seam be finished by hand?

A. Imitation suede garments are hemmed one of two ways—machine stitched or fused into place. While both of these methods are correct, I would never suggest hand sewing the hem in place.

If you want to fuse the hem in position, decide on the new length and leave an extra inch to an inch and a half for the hem. Press the hem carefully from the wrong side; then slip a slightly narrower piece of fusible webbing in the hem and press permanently according to instructions.

The other solution would be to ask a friend who sews well to simply machine stitch two rows of stitching on your dress. This isn't difficult, but must be accurate.

Be sure you never use glue on imitation suede. Since the fabric is synthetic, glue can actually eat it away.

Crepe De Chine

Q. I'm making a dress with polyester crepe de chine. I have so much trouble with the seams puckering. Can you help me?

A. First, understand that any polyester or synthetic fiber will not look as pressed and flat as a natural fiber. Don't use too fine a machine stitch. Try using ten to twelve stitches per inch. A shorter stitch causes too much thread buildup, which can cause puckering.

After stitching a long seam, don't backstitch at the end. After the dress has been removed from the sewing machine, run your fingernail down the seam, easing out any excess fabric as you go along. It doesn't matter if the hem isn't exactly even—perhaps one seam will be as much as ½ inch longer than the other. If this avoids the puckered look, it's important. The hem length can be adjusted when you measure the hem on yourself.

When doing sample stitching before working on your garment, don't use a tiny square of fabric. Instead, find some long strips of scraps and practice on an actual length of the garment.

Water Spots

Q. I was under the impression that 100 percent polyester fabric would not water spot like silk. I recently made a shirt of polyester crepe de chine, and every little drop of water spots the fabric. Did I get a bad piece of fabric, or is this to be expected?

A. Polyester is a miracle fiber, but when used for many different types of fabrics, it gives different results. I don't think it would be possible to spot a polyester knit fabric, but a fine woven fabric is another story.

The fabric you referred to is a fine imitation of pure silk crepe de chine, and it will usually water spot. However, you can wash it and the spots will come out.

I think one has to take advantage of the best qualities of any fabric. In this case, the washability is invaluable. I guess we all have become spoiled with the knits and will have to take a little more care when wearing polyester.

Washing Crepe De Chine

Q. I purchased some lovely polyester crepe de chine for a blouse. The fabric was machine washable and could be dried in the dryer. When I did this, the fabric appeared to have oily spots in it that were very unattractive. I rewashed it in the machine and hung it up on a hanger. It came out perfect. Is it true that this type of fabric shouldn't be placed in the dryer; and if so, why didn't the manufacturer say this specifically?

A. Unfortunately, the washing instructions are almost too general and there are always exceptions. I know exactly what you are speaking about, and the spots are much more noticeable with the darker colors of polyester crepe de chine.

We did some experimenting and finally came up with a cause for the spots. It seems that if you have used an antistatic spray or sheets of antistatic paper in your dryer, some of this clings to the walls of the dryer. When it comes in contact with some of these delicate silklike fabrics, it causes spots.

My advice to you would be to thoroughly rinse out the blouse or whatever in this fabric by hand. Then place on a hanger to dry. If you still want to wash your garments in the washer, remove them and hang up to dry instead of placing in the dryer. I know it will work for you.

Prewash Fabrics

Q. Why must all fabrics today be prewashed?

A. With the washable factor today in most fabrics, we must take the time to prevent disasters later. If you were going to have your garment dry-cleaned, you wouldn't have to bother.

Prewashing prevents later shrinkage, removes chemical odors and also removes excess fabric finishes which sometimes cause your machine to skip stitches. Preshrinking is simple if you baste the selvages together as well as both ends—it's much easier to straighten later.

If you intend to put your finished garment in the clothes dryer, you must also do this with the uncut fabric. It is also a good idea to preshrink your zippers and any trim you will be using. A few minutes' time spent on preshrinking can save disasters and disappointments later.

Washing Prints

Q. I have just had a disaster with cotton fabric that faded, and wonder what I did wrong. I bought a lovely piece of white fabric with dark brown printed designs. I prewashed it, as I do everything that will be washed later. When I got it out to use, the brown design had come off on the white background. I tried washing it again but nothing changed. What could I have done to avoid this?

A. When a deep color contrast is used on a white background, the dye can run if not handled properly. First, when prewashing your fabric, use a little salt or white vinegar in the water. This will set the color and help somewhat.

The second it has completed its cycle, remove it from the washer and immediately place it in the dryer or hang it up to dry. When you let it remain in any position where the color can come off on another area, you are in trouble, especially where you have such deep color contrasts.

You won't ruin good quality fabric unless you allow it to remain in the washer while wet instead of removing it immediately and drying it the proper way. It is not the fault of the fabric, but of improper handling.

Washing Woven Fabrics

Q. I am confused about today's woven fabrics that are marked permanent press, wash and wear, wrinkle resistant or mini-care. I have found almost without exception that these fabrics still need to be pressed. Am I being overly critical or am I doing something wrong when I wash my clothes?

A. Although a lot has to do with the way you wash and dry your clothes, touch-up pressing is usually desired. I would suggest using a fabric softener in the washer and an antistatic agent in the dryer.

Also, a very important rule is to take clothes out of the washer or dryer the minute the cycle is completed. If you leave clothes in your dryer after this point, they acquire new permanent wrinkles that are difficult to remove with any pressing.

Today's fabrics seem like a dream to me. I remember when all washables had to be starched to retain the finish, then sprinkled until they were almost wet. Finally, you spent hours doing your ironing.

I think most garments look better if they are simply touched up with a steam iron. This only takes minutes to do and is well worth the extra effort. Of course, this can be eliminated with most children's clothes as well as casual clothing or sportswear.

Water-Repellent Fabrics

Q. Quite often when reading the fashion pages, I come across water-repellent rain suits, coats, or pants. Yet, it is almost impossible to find fabrics that are actually water-repellent. What can home sewers do?

A. Manufacturers can have any fabric treated for water repellency, but since our needs are more varied, it would be impossible to market a huge variety of such fabrics. However, you may take any fabric that you would like to use for rainwear and make it water-repellent yourself with a spray fabric protector. It comes with full directions included.

I have put this product to other uses that have been very successful—on men's ties, scarves, collars of dresses and even silk shoes. There are very few limitations, but as usual, I would suggest testing a sample piece of your fabric before any application.

Making Ski Clothes

Q. My family is going on a skiing holiday soon. Since the price of ready-to-wear ski clothing is so high, I want to make some of the articles myself. Do you have any tips about water-repellent fabric?

A. Water-repellent fabrics do require a few different sewing techniques that ordinary materials do not, but you can use almost any pattern you like.

Designer touches such as yokes, pockets, collars and unusual fastenings are perfect. Raglan sleeves are easy to handle, but if you choose a pattern with set-in sleeves, you should take a little of the fullness out of the cap of the sleeves since your specially treated fabric makes it impossible to shrink out fullness.

To remove fullness from the sleeve pattern, take a small fold in your pattern at the shoulder mark, extending the fold to about three to four inches deep and tapering to nothing. Then slash the pattern above the notches in front and back of the sleeve and allow the pattern to spread slightly so it will be nice and flat for cutting.

When placing your pattern on the fabric, pin within the seam allowance, as pin marks tend to show in this type of fabric. Also, machine stitch with a fine needle.

It is usually not necessary to use interfacing because of the body of the fabric. If you do, however, I recommend using a woven-type interfacing rather than a fusible-type since fusing is more difficult to use.

Topstitching is attractive and it is recommended that you use two threads in your needle at the same time. If you don't have two spool holders, just place a bobbin on top of a spool and thread the pieces through the needle together. Test stitch actual length and stitching on scraps of fabric to determine what is most pleasing to you before proceeding with your garment. When pressing, be sure to use a synthetic setting on your iron to avoid burning.

Ski garments are fun to make, and you can sure save lots of money by creating your own.

Chapter 5
ULTRASUEDE®

Pattern Selection

Q. I want to make either a suit or coat of Ultrasuede®. However, everything I read about this fabric scares me because it doesn't ease well. What type of pattern can I select?

A. I would suggest patterns that look as though they were made for leather. After all, Ultrasuede® should have leather details, such as rows of topstitching on all the outer edges. I wouldn't suggest a pattern with many gathers or much fullness. If you do have gathers, perhaps you can fold this excess in unpressed tucks or pleats.

The ease at the cap of sleeves would be the only difficult detail to achieve, but with care, this can also be accomplished.

To avoid the cap of sleeves for jackets and coats, try to find a pattern with raglan sleeves. Actually, they are much easier to slip over other sweaters and shirts. The cut is very high, and they aren't loose and sloppy. They fit the arm almost the same as a set-in sleeve.

Many of the new sleeves have a dropped shoulder line. This means the cap of the sleeve isn't as high and is more like the sleeves found on men's clothes. This makes the sleeve much easier to set in because the cap is flatter and has much less fabric to ease in.

Don't be afraid of Ultrasuede®. It is such a joy to use and more of a joy to own. It is almost easier to work on than a woven fabric. Yes, you can even rip it if you make a mistake.

Lining Ultrasuede®

Q. I'm considering purchasing Ultrasuede® to make a coat. I have looked at the ready-made coats and jackets in our better shops and have been shocked to find that most of them are unlined. Would you recommend this type of finishing, or would you line the coat as the pattern suggests?

A. Sometimes you must use your own judgment instead of doing what the manufacturers do. First of all, as we all know, anything that is to be machine washed should be preshrunk. This applies to interfacings, linings and anything we use in construction.

In ready-to-wear, there is an extra problem that we don't have at home. They can't be sure the fabrics have been preshrunk sufficiently, and washing an expensive garment at home could produce disastrous results. Therefore, with ready-made garments, they must avoid every type of problem that may cause a garment to be returned.

Personally, I feel a coat or jacket would be very difficult to slip over dresses, blouses, sweaters or whatever without a lining. If you use a very lightweight lining, such as the polyester called Casino by Skinner, you wouldn't be adding bulk or additional weight to your garment and it would be infinitely more practical. If nothing more, by all means consider lining the sleeves of jackets and coats.

Remember, preshrink any piece of fabric that you intend to wash later. Use the same temperature for the water and the same heat for the dryer. This will avoid many disappointments later.

Combining Fabrics with Ultrasuede®

Q. Can Ultrasuede® fabric be used in combination with any fabrics?

A. Since Ultrasuede® fabric is machine washable and dry-cleanable, I see no reason why it can't be combined with almost any fabric desired. You will need to study the details carefully to be sure you use the fabric in the right areas—not the drapable, full sections, but the stable ones such as collars, cuffs, bandings, yokes and vests.

Because you will be using it in combination with other fabrics, you may not always be able to use the flat or open seam method. It is acceptable to use whatever method of construction fits the situation best. I have even seen two methods of construction used in the same garment.

This is the real joy of sewing—trying unusual combinations and using luxurious fabrics, even if it is in small quantities.

Whether you use the flat or open seam method of construction, be sure to use lots of topstitching to keep all the seams and edges flat and detailed the same as real leather.

Working with Ultrasuede®

Q. Is there more than one quality or thickness of this fabric? What kind of thread should be used? How should the hem be finished, and should seams be pressed open or to one side like the ready-made clothes?

A. There is only one Ultrasuede® fabric, but there are many imitations on the market. Ultrasuede® fabric is distributed by Spring Mills in this country and is forty-five inches wide. You cannot possibly compare it with any other fabric of this kind; the only similarity would be in the suede look and feel. Prices per yard vary in many parts of the country.

As for thread, I personally prefer the 100 percent long staple polyester thread called Metrosene. If this is not available in your area, you may use other brands of polyester thread. I prefer this to poly-cotton thread.

As for the finish of the hems, you may machine stitch them or use Stitch Witchery to bond them in position. Never use glue of any type.

The seams may be pressed open or to one side, but most of them will be topstitched to remain in the desired position. This not only adds detail, but gives you the real leather look that you are emulating.

Yes, a zipper can be used very nicely. Machine buttonholes are usually preferred, mostly because the styling is often the shirt-type fashions that require machine buttonholes and small buttons.

Always pretest your machine stitching on your fabric before beginning. I usually suggest ten to twelve stitches per inch.

Use Correct Needle

Q. I have just finished an Ultrasuede® skirt, but am heartsick because I can't get the holes out of the fabric from where I ripped out some stitching. I used a ball-point needle. What did I do wrong?

A. Unfortunately, a lot of instructions for this marvelous fabric are inaccurate and often written by someone who is writing in theory only, and who hasn't put his instructions to a test.

This fabric should never be stitched with a ball-point needle. The needle has actually punctured the fabric, and it can't be erased.

I have found that a size 11 needle (or a size 70 in a European needle) works perfectly and can be ripped out without showing—provided your stitch length isn't too short.

Never use the heavy buttonhole twist thread for machine topstitching; use your regular thread.

Washing Ultrasuede®

Q. I have finally gotten the courage to make an Ultrasuede® dress. It needs to be cleaned and I can't bring myself to throw away $100 of fabric in the washing machine. Is this fabric really washable?

A. You are having a natural reaction. However, if you have used the real Ultrasuede®, you don't have a thing to worry about. If you followed my instructions for construction, you used washable all-bias Pellon® for your interfacing and all-polyester thread for stitching. Therefore, your garment should be completely washable.

Put it in your washer using a gentle action setting, warm (not hot) water, and any mild soap. Wash it about five minutes and let it spin to remove the moisture.

Place it in your dryer, using a permanent press setting to avoid excessive heat, and watch the time. Don't allow it to get completely dry, and never allow it to remain in your dryer after it has turned off.

Remove it, shake it gently, smooth the collar, cuffs, or fronts, hang on a hanger and let it dry completely.

I have an Ultrasuede® garment in the very impractical off-white shade, but I love it. I can toss it in the washer and dryer and be ready to wear it again in a couple of hours. Believe it or not, I have already washed my own dress a dozen times. I'm convinced it gets more beautiful with every washing.

If you have a garment in the darker colors which won't show the soil, perhaps you will prefer having it dry-cleaned. Ultrasuede® dry-cleans beautifully. Wear it lots and enjoy every minute of it.

Does Ultrasuede® Wear Well?

Q. Do you have any information as to how the nap will last on Ultrasuede® fabric?

A. My own experience is that Ultrasuede® fabric is practically indestructible. I have had a dress for three years that has been washed at least fourteen times, and it is still like new. In fact, I think it is even more attractive than when I made it.

My husband also has an Ultrasuede® fabric jacket that was tailored for him three years ago. It is still like new. He gets many compliments whenever he wears it. Not one sign of wear is on any of the edges.

Ultrasuede® fabric is being used for upholstery, shoes, purses and ready-to-wear garments. It is definitely the fabric of our time. Use it if you can afford it and enjoy it to the fullest. You'll love every minute of it.

Incidentally, I also have seen it used for patches on sleeves, for cuffs and collars on wool garments, and for binding edges of coats that have worn out. This marvelous fabric has practically no limitations, but don't accept something that looks like Ultrasuede® fabric. There are no substitutes. It is worth every penny of the price you pay.

Technique for Set-In Sleeves

Q. I am working with a shirt dress out of Ultrasuede® and am having a terrible time with the set-in sleeves. I have had them in and out several times. I'm afraid one more mistake and I won't be able to rip the stitches without it showing. What is the secret?

A. The problem is with the set-in sleeve which requires easing. It is almost impossible to ease these nonwoven pseudosuedes and leathers. However, there is a technique that will help considerably. First, be sure the sleeve is a true set-in sleeve, and not a drop shoulder sleeveline.

Cut a bias strip of Tri-Dimensional interfacing, the kind that is suggested for ties. Your strip should be about ten to twelve inches long and 1½ inches wide. Place this strip on the wrong side of the sleeve cap beginning at the front notch, over the cap of the sleeve, and to the back notch. Place the edge of the strip at the edge of your sleeve.

Secure stitching at the notch; then pull the bias strip (which is on top) tightly, stretch the strip and hold firmly about two inches from the start, and stitch through both layers of fabric just inside the seamline. Continue the same with the next two inches, pulling the bias tightly, and continue stitching until you have come to the back notch. Part of the bias strip will be left over—simply cut it off.

Notice immediately how beautifully rounded the sleeve cap has become. This should now fit perfectly into the armhole with no gathers or puckers.

Remember: These instructions are for a true set-in sleeve only, and not any kind of drop shoulder design. Yes, it works on any fabric which is difficult to ease. You should have a nice soft cap to the finished sleeve.

Ultrasuede® Jumper

Q. I would like to make a jumper of Ultrasuede®, but would like you to recommend another kind of fabric for the facings to avoid the extra bulk. Do I topstitch around the neck and arms? Should I use a deep hem? I want this to look professional since the fabric is so expensive.

A. First, I suggest you check some of the ready-made garments that are made of Ultrasuede®. You will find they cut the seam allowance off and use the leather method of construction, which is cut edges and lapped seams. Because you are not turning the seams, the same fabric is recommended for the facings. It will not be bulky.

The beauty of this fabric is the detail you achieve with machine stitching. The edges should be stitched as close as possible to the cut edge, and again about ¼ inch in from the first row of stitching. Seams and hem are all doublestitched.

You don't allow a deep hem because it would be too stiff and bulky.

For the belt of the jumper, I suggest you machine stitch several rows of stitching, one each ¼ inch from the last row. This creates a very attractive belt.

Plunge in; you'll be so proud of your jumper. This fabric is simple to sew. True, it is expensive, but it is so practical that you will love it. Wear it always with great pride and joy.

Ultrasuede® Belts

Q. I just completed an Ultrasuede® dress but haven't enough fabric left for the belt. What direction should it be cut?

A. You are in luck. The belt should be cut on the cross-grain so that the nap will be in the same direction as your dress. Since Ultrasuede® is only forty-five inches wide, it will probably be necessary to piece the length, especially if you are using the popular tie version. And remember, the belt must be made double, or it will curl up like a limp piece of fabric.

Usually, the finished width is about two to 2½ inches wide. You will not need any more seam allowances. For piecing at the back, remember that you are imitating leather, so use leather details.

Instead of piecing the back with a straight seam, cut the end at an angle resembling the point and two sides of a triangle. Lap this end over the under layer and topstitch twice. Do the same for the under side.

Next, place the two layers of fabric with wrong sides together (you never stitch and try to turn a belt inside out), pin in place and machine stitch very close to the cut edge. The second stitching should be ¼ inch from the first stitching. This belt can be made very quickly, and remember, it's a great accessory for dresses, jackets, coats, and skirts.

Fig. 6 – Redesigning a Short Dress

Redesigning a Short Dress

Q. Is there any way to lengthen an Ultrasuede® dress? I bought one about three years ago, and now it's about an inch too short. I've tried to match it with new fabric, but it has faded somewhat. Any suggestions?

A. If this was a shirtwaist dress, check the front bands to see if the excess fabric was cut away. If it was, there is nothing for you to do except shorten the dress and make a casual jacket from it. (See figure 6.)

Actually, a shirt dress would make a perfect jacket. Coordinate it with an attractive plaid or patterned fabric for pants or a skirt, and you'll get lots of wear from it.

If it is possible to lengthen the dress, remove all the machine stitching, wash the garment and scrub the hem area extra well, and dry. Usually, you can lengthen it at least an inch or slightly more.

At the point where the original hem was turned up, machine stitch two rows of stitching to cover up the hem marks. Stitch it at the lower edge with two or more rows of stitching.

I have seen this done, and it does work. However, each garment is different, and without actually seeing your dress, I can only offer solutions that have worked for others.

Since so many garments are now made out of chiffon, crepe de chine and wool, and trimmed in Ultrasuede®, perhaps you can cut the dress up and use it for trimmings or a vest rather than lose an entire investment. This is the time to put your creative genius to work.

Chapter 6
CUTTING AND CONSTRUCTION

Before You Cut, Check the Nap

If you are a beginner or a fairly inexperienced sewer, before you begin your sewing project remember to check the nap of the fabric. Nap, in this case, means that the pattern pieces must all be placed on the fabric in the same direction.

You must carefully examine your fabric: Is it a one-way plaid? Does it have a print that must be cut in one direction? Does it actually have a nap such as corduroy or velvet, or is it a knit?

Ordinarily, all knits should be placed in the same direction. This is not as important with your matte jerseys as it is with sweater-type knits. Coatings also have nap and they must be cut the same way.

If the coat fabric is camel's hair, cashmere, a wool blend with hair, or any fabric that has a different texture, depending on the direction you stroke, be sure these fabrics are cut like fur. The fabric should feel smooth from the shoulder down to the hem.

Velvets and corduroys are often cut in the opposite direction, or against the nap, to produce a deeper and richer color—but this is a matter of preference.

If your pattern doesn't have a layout for fabrics with or without nap, check the cutting instruction sheet to see how much extra fabric you will need to cut everything in one direction. Usually, it takes about ½ yard more fabric to allow for the nap. This also depends on the fullness of the skirt.

I can't stress nap too strongly. It's the one giveaway tip to that homemade look instead of the custom-made look. Check your fabric and pattern layout before purchasing fabric and actually cutting it. You can correct almost any error if you discover it before you get your scissors in your hand. After that, it's almost impossible to correct.

Pattern Cutting

Q. My mother always cuts my patterns out for me and then I make them. I would like to cut them myself, but mother says this is the hardest part about sewing. Is this true?

A. You didn't say your age, but since you are questioning this, you are definitely old enough to do your own cutting. I'm sorry, but I don't agree with your mother. I think cutting the pattern is usually the easiest step in construction.

Whether it's easy or hard, it's important that you do it yourself because you can learn so much about the pattern to be assembled. It's also important to know your own figure so that you can add a little here and there for fitting.

My only word of advice is to prepare your fabric before beginning. Preshrink, if necessary. Make sure the grain line is even and straight. If there is a pattern or print, study your fabric to be sure about the areas that need matching.

If possible, I recommend you always cut your pattern in one direction. However, if the skirt is flared at the hem, you can often save fabric by fitting one piece of pattern into the other by using both directions of the fabric.

Ask your mother to let you lay out your own pattern, and then ask her to check it before you cut it. The first thing you know, you will be doing all of this as a routine. Keep up the enthusiasm—sewing can offer a lifetime of pleasure.

Right Side of Wool

Q. I can remember my grandmother telling me that the right side of wool was always on the inside of the fold. Since wools are so difficult to come by today, what is the rule with today's fabrics?

A. The same rule applies about ninety-nine percent of the time. Almost all fabric I have seen is folded with the right side inside. However, it's best to examine both sides carefully and make your own decision and stick with it. You can't use one side and then the other in the same garment without a shadowed effect.

Avoid a Mistake

Q. I recently cut out a dress that called for cutting each piece of the pattern singly instead of folding the fabric and cutting two pieces at a time. I don't know how it happened, but I forgot to turn the pattern over the second time. Much to my unhappiness, I cut two pieces for the same side. How can we avoid this mistake?

A. When it is necessary to cut a garment on a single layer of fabric, it's best to take extra time to cut your second half of the pattern out of another sheet of paper (thus, you would have a right front and a left front, right sleeve and left sleeve, etc). Now you can actually place each and every piece of the pattern on your fabric at once and avoid this error.

Yes, many of us have made this mistake by simply forgetting to turn over the pattern. Believe it or not, I had one student who actually cut the same sleeve out four times before she got it right.

Nap

Q. Please explain the word "nap" given on patterns in reference to the amount of yardage required. I was under the impression that nap meant velvet or corduroy, and I've just ruined a beautiful dress because the cutting instructions showed one piece of the skirt cut in one direction and the other fitted into the fabric, but reversed in direction. Since this was a print that wasn't reversible, the skirt is a disaster. I was able to salvage the bodice and add a solid skirt, but there must be more to cutting than the pattern tells us. Can you explain this?

A. Perhaps the pattern companies should be more specific when they tell us about nap. Actually, the word is used to describe any fabric that has a one-way design as well as fabric with a nap, such as velvets, cashmeres, and knits. Many plaids must also be placed in one direction.

Check your pattern layout before making a purchase. It is often necessary to purchase an extra length for the skirt. Remember, even knits that are a solid color have a direction and must be cut with all pieces of your pattern placed in the same direction.

Cutting Corduroy

Q. Is it possible to use any other grain besides the lengthwise grain in the corduroy?

A. It is true—corduroy must all be cut in the same direction. Therefore, when checking the cutting instructions as well as the amount of fabric you will need, you must use the yardage requirements for fabric WITH NAP.

However, there are many variations you can use with your corduroy, and they are most attractive. I have seen jackets with the cross-grain used instead of lengthwise, and it gives them a completely different look—very unique.

For skirts, I would suggest a bias skirt pattern that has four gores. Cut the pieces according to the fabric layout for NAP and forget the lengthwise wale of the corduroy. The four seams will end up like a V or chevron effect and be most attractive.

It's fun to experiment with fabrics and create new effects. Just think twice before cutting to see that it is a workable design. Naturally, when your pattern calls for fabrics with nap and you are using a flared skirt pattern, you will need extra fabric because you can't fit the pieces of the pattern into one another.

However, you won't need to waste any fabric. Just think of something else to do with those unused areas. A vest would be perfect. If you only have enough fabric for the front, you can use another fabric for the back. You could use scraps for pillows, purses or whatever.

Cutting Knits

Q. When you tell us that knits should be cut in the same direction, do you mean the actual cutting, or do you mean the way the pattern is placed on the fabric?

A. All the pieces of your pattern must be placed in the same direction on your knit fabric. Knits do have direction; if you place the pattern pieces on the fabric as you would when the pattern layout calls for "without nap," you would have a distinct shading of your fabric. Actually, if at all possible, it is much better if you can place all your pattern pieces in the same direction. This will save any error in cutting.

As to actually cutting the fabric with your scissors, it doesn't matter what angle you use. The important factor is the way the pattern is placed on the fabric.

How to Match Plaids

Q. I have fallen in love with a lovely plaid woolen fabric and want to use it to make a jacket. The only thing that is stopping me is matching plaids. Can you give me a few simple tips about matching plaids?

A. Plaids can be so beautiful, and they really aren't as much a problem as you would imagine if you can just remember one thing: Plaids are matched in the cutting stage, not when sewing.

First, be sure the plaid is absolutely even. I suggest pinning it on the foldline after checking to be sure the fold is on the exact center of a block in the plaid or on a center line. This should be done on a large table, your carpet or anyplace that won't permit the fabric to slip.

Fold back the top layer of fabric to about six inches from the fold; then carefully lay it down, shifting the fabric, if necessary, so that all vertical and horizontal lines are even. Fold down another six inches, and continue until you have come to the selvages. It isn't necessary to pin all these lines if you are sure the fabric didn't slide out of line.

Now your big job is finished. The rest is easy if you just remember a few key points. Begin with the center front or back, placing it on the center of a block (or a center line). Next, you will match any notch BELOW the bustline to the notch on the next section, and continue to the back. In other words, the horizontal lines should match. Because of the shaping, the squares will not be exactly even; this isn't important.

Last, when cutting the sleeves, be sure the notch at the front of the sleeves matches the notch at the front of the armhole.

Plaids are beautiful, and they're not as difficult as you imagine.

Matching Plaids on Jackets

Q. You mention that plaids must match horizontally around the jacket as well as the sleeves. I have recently taken a sewing class where the instructor said the upper sleeve could not be matched due to the ease. Is it possible to match the sleeve?

A. I have found that if you match the single front notch of the sleeve with the single front notch of the armhole of your jacket, you will have a horizontal plaid that will match almost perfectly, except perhaps at the extreme top of the sleeve. Since the ease of the sleeve begins at the notch and continues up to the shoulder, the most obvious part of the sleeve will carry your eye straight across the jacket and continue to the sleeve.

It is rare that the back of the jacket will match as well since the sleeve is cut in one. I think it is far more important to match the front and let the back take care of itself.

Even Plaids for Bias Skirts

Q. Do some plaids make a better bias skirt than others? The one I just made didn't come out the way I wanted it to at the center front and back.

A. For a perfect chevron at the center front and back of a bias skirt, the plaid should be an even plaid. That means that the blocks of the plaid should form a perfect square. If they don't, it's better to use a pattern without a center front or back seam—just side seams where you will also apply your zipper closing.

Bias Seaming

Q. What causes bias seams to draw up? I have tried to avoid patterns that have any bias on them. However, I have fallen in love with a bias-cut evening dress, but am afraid to try it because I never have any luck with this type of seaming.

A. Three things could be causing your difficulty with bias seaming. First, never underline a bias-cut garment. The two layers of fabric cannot hang even. If you need a lining, use a separate lining instead of attaching it in the seams of the garment fabric.

Second, never use your sewing machine to zigzag the edges of the seams. The machine tends to pull up the fabric, which will cause it to pucker and not lay smoothly after it has been seamed. I might remind you that the bias seams don't ravel as do ones cut on the straight grain. However, if you feel your fabric does need seam finishing, overcast the edges by hand. Keep your stitches rather far apart and looser; it works perfectly.

The third point to remember is to pull seams that have been cut on the bias as you stitch. If you don't pull as you stitch, the seams will break the thread in order to gain the stretch all bias should have. Point to remember: Don't do anything to keep your seams from stretching as they are stitched. If you follow these points, you will be more than happy with the results.

Zipper on Bias

Q. I am making a bias skirt with the zipper closing in the center back. No matter how hard I try, I simply can't apply this zipper without distorting the fabric. What can I do?

A. The solution is a simple one and the only one that works for me. Change the position of the zipper and place it in the side seam where the fabric is more on grain than at the center back.

An application of this type is possible to do on the bias, but it takes time and patience.

I have found that when you do try this zipper on the bias, it's best to have the seams meet at the center of the zipper instead of the lapped application. You must also pull the fabric as you baste it to the zipper tape. However, if possible, take the easier route and change the position to the side seam. It will make no difference in the overall construction.

Fig. 7 — Unlined Coat

Use Wider Seams for Unlined Coat

Q. Please give me a little more information on the construction technique of the unlined coat. You say to use a seam 1¼ inches wide on all inner construction. Does this show on the pattern pieces or must you add this on your own?

A. Almost any kind of pattern for a jacket or coat would be used in the unconstructed, unlined method of construction. Because the pattern will be designed for standard construction, you will have to make the necessary changes to your own pattern.

I suggest the wider seams for your inner seams because of the flat-felled finish you will be using to encase the cut or raw edges of your seams. Since your fabric will be much heavier than dress weight, it would be too difficult to work with only 5/8-inch seams.

If you are binding the outer edges, you will cut the 5/8-inch seam allowance off entirely before you begin your binding; otherwise, the finished edges would be wider than the pattern called for.

In the unlined garment, as well as a garment made from leather or difficult fabrics, try to find a pattern with raglan sleeves, as they eliminate many problems. (See figure 7.)

Interfacing Placement

Q. Does it make any difference in the neckline of a dress if you put the interfacing on the wrong side of the material as the pattern says, or if you put it on the facing and then attach it to the neckline?

A. This construction detail would depend entirely on the type of interfacing you are using. I have always liked to place the interfacing on the wrong side of the fabric because I think it stabilizes the fabric much better than if it is applied to the facing.

I would suggest you stitch your shoulder seams together and then apply the interfacing. You would overlap the interfacing at the shoulders instead of stitching it in with the shoulder seam, which often would make the shoulder seam too thick and bulky.

My favorite interfacing for most dresses is the featherweight all-bias Pellon®. This gives body without bulk.

There is another alternative, however, which would include the press-on type of facing. You must check your fabric first by pressing some of this interfacing on a scrap to see if it shows through, which would be most unattractive. With press-on interfacing, it is usually recommended that you apply this to the facings instead. This would avoid any chance of it showing through.

The press-on interfacings come in different weights. For dresses, use only the very lightweight. This is a quick interfacing. However, I must caution you that it is also very easy to pull the fabric out of shape while you are applying the interfacing. Handle with care, and be aware of the fact that it is very important to retain the exact shape of the pattern.

Warp Knits

Q. I fell in love with a beautiful border print in a knit fabric. Because of the border, the garment would have had to be cut on the cross-grain of the fabric instead of the lengthwise grain. I tried to test the stretch of the fabric, and it honestly didn't seem to stretch in either direction. Because of this, would it be all right to cut it on the cross-grain?

A. Your fabric must have been a warp knit, since you say it didn't have any stretch in either direction. This knit is very easy to work with because it resembles a woven piece of fabric, and thus, is stabilized. Yes, it could be cut in either direction.

For those of you who are looking for the kind of knits that won't cling too closely to the figure, remember to look for these marvelous warp knits. They are especially advisable for the larger figure, and they are very easy to work with.

Neckline and Armhole on Knits

Q. Is it possible to finish the neckline and armholes of a knit garment without a facing? I have looked at the ready-mades, and they have a row of zigzag stitching along the neckline and armholes. The fabric is cut close to the stitching and there is no facing. This seems like a way to eliminate a lot of extra work and bulk.

A. This is a new way of construction with knits and sheer knits. Because the knit fabric is flexible, it recovers after it has been stretched. You may turn the seam allowance over and use a large zigzag stitch as a decorative finish for the neckline. This zigzag stitch keeps the neckline flexible. A straight stitch would probably break with any undue pressure from stretching.

These garments are dependent on the knit's stretch factor for the ease of slipping on and off. It also eliminates the need for a zipper. These types of clothing were designed for the gals with rather small measurements. Not everyone can wear these figure-clinging garments.

Use Elastic on Neckline Corners

Q. When I wear a dress with a low, square neckline, the neckline doesn't stay nice and flat. Instead, it gapes and isn't attractive. Is there any way to keep this neckline close to my body?

A. Yes, there is a way and it is rather simple. It isn't necessary to do this with high necklines as they will stay in place.

When the neckline is a perfect square and cut lower, you can attach elastic to the corners and hook it in back. Use a narrow elastic, no wider than ½ inch, and fasten it by hand to the inside corner of each side of the neckline over the facing on the wrong side of the garment.

Hand sew both sides of elastic for about ½ inch. Try the dress on, slip the two loose ends of elastic under your bra straps around to your back, and mark with a pin where the hook and eye should be applied. Don't pull the elastic too tight or it will destroy the appearance of the dress. At the center back, apply a small hook to one end of the elastic and an eye to the other. You'll find the dress will look perfectly smooth in front and the square neckline will not gape, but will stay in place the way you hoped it would.

Buttonholes

Q. How can I decide whether to make machine buttonholes or bound buttonholes? I want my garments to look professional.

A. First, it depends on the style of the garment; second, on the fabric.

Today, with the shirt-look and the small buttons by the dozen, I prefer a beautifully made machine buttonhole to the bound buttonholes.

If you are making a lovely suit or coat, machine buttonholes would spoil it. In that case, practice until you have a perfect bound buttonhole. They will give your garments a truly professional custom finish.

If your fabric ravels easily, you may find it necessary to press on a small patch of press-on interfacing on the wrong side of each buttonhole. Also, when you sew your welts to the fabric, take very small stitches and backstitch frequently to catch all the threads.

Use Wrong Side of Wool

Q. I have selected a beautiful plaid fabric for a suit for fall. The fabric has a brushed look, and I'm not sure I like this. The wrong side of the wool looks beautiful and smooth. Can I safely use the wrong side instead of the right side?

A. Most wools can be used on either side, especially the better quality fabrics. Check the wrong side carefully. This is where you would find the yarns tied or find any flaws in the yarns. If it is perfect, there is no reason you can't reverse the fabric.

The brushed or napped surface is very popular. If you use the brushed side, be sure to cut all pieces of your pattern in one direction with the nap. In other words, the nap should be smooth as you run your hand from the shoulder down to the hem.

Dart Pucker

Q. I am working with a jacket that has raglan sleeves and a shoulder seam that ends in a dart at the end of the shoulder. There is a definite pucker at the end of this dart and it looks terrible. How can I correct this?

A. Often, the dart is not tapered enough for every individual. Try ending the dart in a slight curve and be sure it is tapered very fine to the end.

This pucker happens if your shoulders are slightly curved or narrow, so each individual will find it necessary to change this dart according to her own shoulder measurements. This is a very simple adjustment to make.

Split Seams

Q. I just finished a pair of expensive wool gabardine slacks and was shocked to find that the seam had actually split the first time I had worn the pants. Is woven fabric sometimes faulty or did I do something wrong in construction?

A. It is very difficult to imagine what your problem is since I haven't seen your slacks. However, I will give you a few hints.

First, you spoke of woven wool gabardine fabric. This is probably the most sturdy fabric ever made, so the problem is not with the fabric.

Perhaps you have been used to making knit pants and didn't allow enough ease for your woven fabric. This is something all of you must learn to watch when changing over from knits to wovens.

Another tip is the width of your seams. I personally prefer one-inch seams in any fabric that will be used where there is some stress and strain, such as pants. NEVER, under any circumstances, cut the seam allowance off close to the stitching line. There is not enough stability to the seam to handle any pull.

Another possibility is the machine needle and the stitch setting. For woven fabrics, never use a ball-point needle—it pierces the fabric and weakens it. Also, never use a stretch stitch for the seam. This also weakens the fabric.

At one time, machine stitching was a simple thing. We only had one stitch and only one kind of machine needle. It is very important today to keep your machine needles carefully marked to avoid using the wrong ones for your fabric. Just think a minute before you begin your sewing—you can save many disappointments later.

Rounded Collar

Q. I have been noticing shirts with rounded instead of pointed collars. Most patterns still show the pointed ones. Is it possible to change my favorite pattern?

A. It is true, many of the new shirts have the Peter Pan collars with the rounded ends. However, the pointed ones are still very classic and as good as they ever were.

Simply take your pattern, carefully round off the end of the collar and mark the new cutting line with a pencil. When it is even, this will be your new pattern. Changing a pattern slightly doesn't take a pattern drafter, just a little courage and common sense.

Blouson Bodice

Q. I have just completed a beautiful print dress with a blouson bodice. I am so discouraged I could cry. The back of the bodice bulges out and there is no blouson at the waistline—the zipper prevents this. Was this pattern designed wrong or am I doing something wrong?

A. I think I know the pattern you are referring to, and I honestly must agree with you—the results are disappointing. No matter how thin the zipper is, the fabric will not blouse as softly once the zipper is applied.

I feel that all blouson patterns should either have a drawstring-type waistline or use elastic. To be able to slip the dress over your head, you would need a zipper that is long enough to allow the dress to slip on, usually about twelve inches.

If the bodice is blouson and the skirt is straight, I have also seen two separate zippers used. The one for the bodice of the dress is stitched only to the waistline, and the excess seven inches hangs loose below the waist. Then a separate skirt zipper is applied to the skirt. This works fairly well.

Reinforcement on Pockets

Q. I have trouble with pockets tearing holes in shirts and jackets at the top corners. I have stitched them twice, but they still tear the garments. There is no way to repair them without a mended spot showing. What am I doing wrong?

A. Remedying this is easier than you can imagine. This little tip will work about 100 percent of the time, unless, of course, there is an abnormal amount of strain on the pockets.

On the wrong side of your garment, place a one-inch square of fabric over the marks of the top corners of your pockets. Baste in place. Now when you machine stitch the pockets, there will be an extra reinforcement at the corners that should help with any normal amount of strain involved.

I'm very much in favor of these reinforcements wherever there is any extra pull or stress. The little patch won't show, and it can save many hours of repair. I would suggest doing the same for a slit neckline, the top of pleats or slits in skirts, and any gusset-type details.

Elastic Waist

Q. What is your opinion of elastic in the waistline of pants and skirts instead of a zipper?

A. This would depend on two things: your figure and the fabric of the pants or skirt. If you are talking about a knit fabric, because of the stretch factor, the elastic will work without causing too much bulk. If you are speaking about a woven fabric, in order to get it over your hips, the waistline would have to be very large. Then when you use elastic, the fabric would bunch up and give your waistline a less than slim look.

Why not combine the zipper and elastic in woven fabrics? You can eliminate darts and use this amount of ease for the elastic. With the addition of the zipper, you would also have the ease you need for slipping your garment on and off. Besides, you have an extra advantage, since most of us fluctuate constantly in our weight. The elastic will assure a perfect fit if you gain or loose a few pounds.

Add Zipper

Q. Many of the patterns that call for knit fabrics don't require or suggest the application of a zipper. Since I'm still old-fashioned enough not to want to mess my hair when I take a dress on or off, is there anything wrong with adding a zipper?

A. Ordinarily, the application of a zipper will not change the lines of the pattern at all. If there is not a seam at the center back, you must be sure to add one for the zipper. If there is a seam, just apply the zipper as you normally do.

When a zipper is not suggested for knits, it is usually because the neckline is either scooped, a V-neck or a boat neck, and there is barely enough room for a zipper. The give of the knit is usually enough to allow the garment to stretch over your head without too much difficulty.

By all means, change any pattern to fit your own individual needs. One of the good points about making your own clothes is that they immediately become custom-made to your own specifications.

Fig. 8 — Using Seam Tape

Using Seam Tape

Q. I recently made a knit blouse that has raglan sleeves. (See figure 8.) I remember you said to apply seam tape to the shoulder seam to avoid stretching, as the sleeve seam is an extension of the shoulder. I applied the tape to the entire length of the sleeve, but it drew up and appeared too tight. What went wrong?

A. You must stitch knits the same way you stretch bias seams—never hold them in. Instead, keep the fabric taut and pull it slightly as you stitch. You must give the seams the same elasticity the fabric has or they will pull up and the stitches will break with the slightest strain.

As for reinforcing, place the seam tape on the shoulder (about four inches only, which is approximately the width of your actual shoulder). Never place the tape in any other area.

If the knit garment has a waistline, you may wish to add the tape to the waist to stabilize the seam because of the extra pull. Be careful, though, to proceed cautiously when using tape on any seam and be sure you aren't restricting the design or fit of the garment.

Seam Finishes

Q. I've just finished a sheer dress that pulls up on all the seams. Before I stitched the seams, I machine overcasted all the raw edges to keep the fabric from raveling. Could this be the reason the seams are drawing up?

A. Machine overcasting the seams of any fabric before stitching the seams could cause trouble, depending on your sewing machine. I rarely find a sewing machine that can overcast a single layer of fabric without pulling the edges up too tight, causing the pucker.

If the fabric looks like it will ravel excessively, you might want to HAND overcast the raw edges. This doesn't really take too much time. Your stitches can be quite large. Just be sure you don't pull your threads too tightly. For most sheer fabrics, make a standard seam stitching, and then without pressing the seam open, make a second stitching about ⅛ inch from the first. You can now cut your excess fabric from the seams fairly close to the second stitching without fear of raveling out.

Most women have a tendency to overconstruct, which changes the effect of construction. The less machine stitching you do when it comes to seam finishes, the better off you are. Unless your sewing machine automatically adjusts the tension to the weight of the thread and the weight of the fabric, try not to use your overcast stitch or zigzag on woven fabrics.

Chapter 7
FITTING AND ALTERATIONS

Pattern Size

Q. I'm still confused about the size of pattern to purchase. My measurements simply aren't the same as those printed on the pattern envelope. If I buy a pattern to fit my bust, it is too tight in the hips; and the opposite is true if I buy a pattern to fit my hips.

What is the easiest way to adjust a pattern?

A. It happens to all of us. Just when you're sure you know your size, you will suddenly purchase a pattern with completely different styling, and then you wish you had chosen a smaller size.

It's best to choose the pattern closest to your chest measurement. If you are one inch larger than the pattern sizing, choose a pattern one size smaller. Of course, if your bust is extremely large and your back is narrow, you will need to make additional corrections to your pattern.

Somehow, most pattern companies don't understand the figure of a gal over thirty years of age. They are usually thicker through the waistline and larger in the hips. This is a simple adjustment to make.

Simply divide the extra width you need by four (for the four side seams), and add to the side seams only. Begin with nothing at the armhole and gradually enlarge to the hip area. From that point to the hem, add the same width as the hips.

Because the style of garments is so different, I never recommend you complete your garment without fitting it. Perhaps you don't care for the amount of ease that was designed into the pattern. We all have different shapes, so we must do some personal adjustments for the most becoming line for each individual.

Fuller Bust

Q. How can I adjust the bustline darts on a size-sixteen pattern that was drafted for a size-ten bust?

A. This is a problem for many women since patterns are cut for the B-cup size. Also, most patterns fail to note that the fuller or larger the bust, the deeper the shaping darts should be.

There is one very good sewing aid on the market that is a great help when altering bustline designs. This device, Adjust-A-Dart, is distributed by Fashionetics, Inc., and you should be able to find it in most fabric shops and notions departments.

To add one word of advice, for fuller busts it is usually necessary to lower the bustline shaping darts. Hence, you must measure from the shoulder to the largest part of your bust and use this as a guide to your new darts.

Bustline Darts

Q. I'm not an experienced seamstress. In fact, I recently learned to sew using knits and have only made things that don't require fitting. Now, on my first encounter with woven fabric, I've been confronted with disaster.

The dress I am making has darts for fitting the bustline, and I'm sure they aren't in the right place. However, I followed the pattern exactly. Can you help me?

A. People who learned to sew using knits will find there is a whole new world waiting with woven fabrics, and the sewing techniques used will be very different.

The most important thing to remember is that you must learn to depend on darts and ease for fitting, and not the stretch factor of knitted fabrics. Also, the placement of bustline darts must be adjusted to the individual woman—the pattern should only suggest location.

To find out where your darts belong, measure yourself from the shoulder to the tip of the bust and compare this measurement with the placement of the dart on the pattern. A side dart should be placed so its point is opposite the fullest part of your bust. If the dart is below the bust, it should end ½ to one inch below the fullest part of your bust.

For your first attempt at a fitted garment, it might be a good idea to baste the darts and try on the garment before you machine stitch the dart.

Making a Pattern Smaller

Q. What is the easiest way (if any) to reduce the bust size from a thirty-six to a thirty-four on a princess dress or jumper pattern? I am rather thick through the back and lower shoulder section, so I need all the room I can have in back.

A. Place the section of your pattern called the side front on a table. Carefully draw a line from shoulder to hem on the straight grain, using the grain mark on your pattern as a guide. Fold the pattern on the line (you may have to experiment to see how much extra room there really is). I would begin by making a ¼-inch fold, which would take out ½ inch on each side or one inch in the front.

Your front shoulder seam will now be more narrow than the back. If the shoulder width was correct, you will have to slit the pattern from the shoulder down about seven inches and separate from shoulder to nothing at the end of slash to give you the extra width to match the back.

Usually, if you are very small across the front, the pattern will also be too wide at the shoulder in front. If this is the case, leave the shoulder narrow and make an extra fold to resemble a small dart at the back of the shoulder in the pattern only, and shoulder seams will match.

Bust Measurements

Q. According to my measurements, I'm using the right size pattern, yet every pattern pulls across the bustline, especially if it has sleeves. Nothing I do seems to help. Can you?

A. Taking the measurement of your bust and buying the pattern that is closest to this measurement is only the beginning. Every figure is different. You might be narrow across the back and full in the bust, which would account for the fit you are getting from your dresses and blouses.

In order to get extra fabric in the front only, separate your pattern by marking it from shoulder to hem at the center between the neckline and the arms' eye. Separate the pattern about ½ inch at the shoulder and taper to nothing just above the waistline. This will give you one extra inch at the front of your pattern only, just where you need it.

You have one more step to take care of. You must take this extra width out of your shoulder line, or the front won't line up with the back. On your paper pattern, take a small fold or dart in the width you have added. In this case, make the fold ¼ inch wide. When you double that, it will eliminate ½ inch. This fold or dart should taper to nothing about seven inches below the shoulder.

You have now added the extra width where you needed it, and the shoulder remains the same as the original pattern. Patterns are merely a starting point. We must alter them to fit our own measurements.

Adding Bustline Dart

Q. I bought a pattern for a wraparound blouse to be used for knits only, and there is no bustline dart. Since I wear a size forty, I do need these darts. How can I add them to my pattern?

A. First, I wouldn't suggest a wrap blouse for anyone who is large in the bust for the simple reason that it will always gape, since there is no way to keep it closed firmly in the front.

If you have already cut out the pattern, try on the blouse. Pin the center fronts over each other and you will probably see a bulge of fabric at the front side seam opposite the largest part of your bust. This is the exact spot where you should pin or mark your dart.

The depth will be determined by the amount you pinch up in your fingers in order to make the sides smooth. Extend your dart to the tip of the bust.

By taking this fabric from the side seams, it will be necessary to shorten the back of the bodice so the side seams come out even. If you are long-waisted in front due to the size of your bust, it might be necessary to lengthen the front only. The dart at the side seam would then make the length of the bodice from underarm to waist the same in the front and back.

For anyone with a large bust, I would suggest you choose a pattern with a zipper. This will eliminate the pull that often occurs with the spaces between buttons, and also eliminate the gaping of the bodice if there is no closing at all.

Changing V Neck

Q. What is the easiest way to change a V neckline and bring it up higher? I find this type of neckline very flattering but always cut too low for me.

A. Place another piece of paper under the front of your pattern. Join it with tape. If you know how much you want to raise the neckline, place a mark at this point at the center front. Using a ruler for an accurate cutting line, place one edge at your new mark at the center front and the other end at the shoulder seamline. Draw a straight line between these two points.

Don't forget to make the same change on your facings. Since all patterns vary in the depth of the neckline, it's better to cut it a little higher. If it's too high, it's simply a matter of stitching lower. However, it's more difficult to make it higher without changing the pattern.

Change Round Neck

Q. Is it possible to change a round neckline to a V neckline? Also, how would I make the facings fit the new neckline?

A. It is easier than you imagine to change a pattern, especially the change you want to make.

Hold the pattern up to your body and check the depth of the new neckline and the width at the shoulder. When you have determined your new neckline, draw a straight line on your pattern between the center front and the shoulder.

Next, cut a sample pattern out of paper with your new neckline and actually pin it at the shoulder seam to the bodice back before trying it on. Remember, a seamline taken off this pattern will make it much lower. When you are completely satisfied with the new pattern, cut the facing from this and you can be sure it will fit perfectly.

Uneven Skirt

Q. I just completed a skirt that is fairly straight with six pleats at the center front. The skirt looks perfect when I'm not wearing it. However, when I put it on, the skirt hangs down in front and the pleats spread out at the hem. Can I correct this?

A. This happens often with pleats at the front of a skirt. It is usually caused by the weight of the excess fabric in the pleat area. Try raising the front of your skirt slightly until it does hang nice and straight.

You might also check to see if the waistband is tight on the skirt. If it fits loosely, it could cause the skirt to hang unevenly. This is a very simple problem and takes seconds to correct.

Sleeve Adjustment

Q. I have developed a very heavy upper arm since my mastectomy. My sleeve patterns are never large enough, and it's virtually impossible to purchase ready-made dresses or blouses that will fit my arm. How can I alter my patterns?

A. You are right—I'm overdue to give you some adjustment tips for your sleeves. If you only have this problem on one arm, cut your one sleeve according to the pattern, and then make a new pattern for the sleeve that needs adjustment.

Draw a vertical line on your pattern from the shoulder to the end of the sleeve.

Place your pattern over another piece of paper, spreading the pattern at the top about one inch and tapering to nothing at the lower part of the sleeve. You can add about ½ inch to each side seam of the sleeve, again tapering to nothing.

Be sure to remember that when you change the underarm seam of the sleeve, you must also add to the side seam of your garment so the sleeve will fit the armhole.

With these adjustments, make a sample sleeve out of lightweight fabric. Actually baste it to the armhole and try it on. You will immediately be able to see if you have added enough or too much, and can make adjustments accordingly.

Once you have made a successful pattern, you can use it as a guide for all your sewing.

Neckline Too Large

Q. I have worked out the size of the pattern for myself with one exception. If the garment has a round neckline, it is always too large. If I get a size smaller, the neckline is perfect but I have to alter the rest of the garment. What should I do?

A. Your problem is quite common and there are several solutions.

The easiest solution is to mark the shoulder seam a little deeper at the neckline. If you reduce the size by ⅛ inch, this will make the neckline ½ inch smaller. Or, you may add ⅛ to ¼ inch all around to make the opening smaller. In either case, you must change the facing or the collar to conform with the garment.

If the neckline of the pattern is too small, do the opposite to make it slightly larger.

You should always remember that the fit of a pattern can't be determined by the sketch on its envelope. Once you work out a perfect fit, don't take any more chances. Use the corrected pattern as a guide for all similar patterns.

Change Neck Size

Q. I am making a robe for my mother and the neck is too tight. How can I change this neckline so the Peter Pan collar will close?

A. To change the size of the neckline, you must proceed cautiously. I would suggest trimming about ¼ inch away from the entire neckline of the robe. Then, trim away the same amount from the neck edge of the collar.

The ¼ inch doesn't sound like much, but it makes a great difference and I wouldn't recommend trimming more than this until you have actually tried it on. If it is still too tight, you can trim a little deeper, but remember the neckline of the collar must be trimmed the same amount.

Pants Length

Q. Is there some way to make pants look good with both the new higher heels and low heels? They seem to be either too long or too short.

A. This is a problem, and there doesn't seem to be any real answer for you. However, if you wear pants all the time, why not make two pair instead of one for each jacket. Did you know that with cutting parts of your pattern separately, you can actually make two pair of pants from three lengths of fabric instead of four?

Be sure when cutting any part of your pattern separately that you reverse the pattern when cutting it the second time. If you are making one pair of pants from forty-five-inch width fabric, open the fabric and cut each piece separately. You will end up with one wide piece of fabric that can be used for a vest or a child's pair of shorts.

As soon as you become more skilled with sewing, you would be surprised how much fabric you can actually save with careful cutting.

Lengthen Crotch Seam

Q. Is there any way to lengthen the crotch seam of purchased slacks? The length of mine is perfect, but the crotch seam is uncomfortably short.

A. This isn't much of an alteration. In fact, it's much easier to fix than slacks with a too-long crotch seam. All you have to do is restitch the seam.

Starting where the curve begins in front, taper your new seam about ½ inch lower than the original seam before curving up to meet the original seam in back. Clip the original seam to release the fabric and your slacks should fit perfectly.

This adjustment will not change the overall length of the slacks.

Shorten Pants with Cuffs

Q. Professionally made pants have such nice cuffs that when I disturb them to shorten my pants, I can never get such a nice cuff again. Is there a way to shorten the cuffs just one inch and not remove the cuff?

A. You are lucky since you only need to shorten the pants one inch. You could actually shorten them two inches without taking out the cuffs—simply take a fold just below the top of the cuffs on the inside of the pants.

If you have to shorten them more than two inches, make a seam just below the top of the cuffs and cut out the excess length.

With the permanent press fabrics, it is very difficult to remove the original press marks and equally difficult to press a new cuff as well as the original.

Rounded Back Adjustment

Q. I've just recently taken up sewing and completed an excellent class in fitting and sewing. I must admit that until this class, I was never aware of the importance of fitting. Now I notice how many poorly fitted garments are around. My pet peeve is the way jackets always seem to pull up at the center back and stand away from the body on an older woman. Is this caused by posture or construction?

A. Unfortunately, as a woman ages, she often develops a high, rounded back, especially if she is a little overweight. It also can be caused by poor posture.

If you are lucky enough to do your own sewing, there is an alteration that is fairly simple to disguise this figure problem.

Slash your back pattern horizontally about four inches below the neckline, beginning at the center back and ending the slash about an inch from the armhole. Place your pattern on a piece of tissue paper, pinning the lower half of the bodice to the paper. Spread the slash about ½ to one inch depending on the curve of the body. Pin this upper section to the tissue. Redraw the center back seam straight to preserve the grain line. Now, add a small dart at the neckline to remove the excess fabric, which will also allow for a better fit because it will bring the neckline back to its original size.

You will notice the bodice or jacket back will now have the extra fabric needed to accommodate the body curve. Consequently, the hem will be straight instead of hiking up at the center back.

One Hip Higher Than the Other

Q. I have one hip that is higher than the other, causing my skirt hems to ride up. This also happens when I wear slacks. I recently went to a sewing clinic, but they didn't help with my individual problem. Also, since I am short, could you please tell me how long a jacket should be for me?

A. For the problem of one hip being much higher than the other, your adjustment must be made at the waistline of the pants or skirts before applying the waistband. Never adjust this at the hemline.

The simplest way to adjust your pattern is to make a basic pattern out of horizontally striped fabric or make your own horizontal lines on a solid fabric. This will show how much fabric needs to be added to accommodate the high hip, since the grainline must remain straight. When you see how much is needed, it will actually be curved up gradually from center front to one side and center back to the same side.

It is best to cover up this adjustment with straight jackets or overblouses. As to the length of jackets for you, this would depend entirely on your proportions, not just your height. It could vary for each of us.

The best way is to experiment by folding up your pattern at different lengths and trying it on over the pants or skirt you will be wearing.

You must have pleasing proportions or you will emphasize either your weight or your height. Perhaps a good friend can help by giving her opinion. Once you find the right length for you, forget what each pattern suggests and adjust the pattern accordingly.

Fabric Not Wide Enough

Q. I finally had the courage to make a skirt of imitation suede, but my wrap skirt pattern doesn't have side seams and the fabric isn't wide enough. Have you a solution?

A. There are two solutions. First, there must be a large dart at the sides for fitting, so you could slash your pattern from the center of these darts clear to the end and separate the two pieces 1¼ inches. This would take care of your two seam allowances. When stitching the seam, you will gradually follow the curve for the original dart.

The second solution is to place your pattern on the cross-grain of the fabric. I have done this and it works beautifully. Of course, you must remember that when you change the grainline of any fabric, you must cut all pieces in the same direction.

One last tip on stitching darts in synthetic suede is to place a circle the size of a quarter of fusible interfacing on the wrong side of the fabric, centering it with the end of the dart. When stitching the dart, you must taper the end as narrow as possible, actually stitching through the interfacing for a smoother effect.

If you wish to press the dart open, you might slash it through the center to within about one inch of the pointed end; then slip a small strip of Stitch Witchery under each edge of the dart and press to hold in place.

Curved Waistband

Q. I am swaybacked because of a spine curvature, and consequently have difficulty fitting waistbands to skirts and pants. I have tried folding out some fabric just below the waistband, but because of full hips, I really need this fabric. Can you help?

A. One of the most successful answers to this question is your choice of pattern. I would recommend a curved waistband instead of a straight one. This waistband actually fits the curve of your hips and doesn't extend above the waistline. It curves lower in the back, which eliminates some of the extra fabric that is found on most patterns.

Gathered Skirt Waistband

Q. I have just finished making a skirt that is almost straight, yet has a few gathers at the waistline. These gathers at the waist seem to make the skirt fit over my curves better than a skirt with darts. However, after I attached the waistband, the gathers billow up almost above the waistband. What should I do?

A. This sounds like your waistband is too tight.

You should always fit the waistband separately from the skirt—don't go by the pattern measurement. You often need more room to tuck in blouses. When cutting the waistband, measure your waist and add about two inches until the skirt has been fitted.

If you do this, I think you will find the waistband fits nicely without stretching, and the skirt will be beautiful on you.

Extra Width for Hips

Q. I have an extra large derriere; it juts out in back like a shelf and I have trouble fitting skirts. It seems that the side seams always pull to the back, and no matter how much I add to allow for my measurements, the seams are never exactly at the sides. Can you help me with this adjustment?

A. First, we must understand that all seams do not need to be changed when we adjust our patterns. In your case, you should add only to the BACK seams, not the side front. This will give you the extra width in the hip area that you need.

In order to fit in at the waist, you may need to make your darts slightly deeper in back (since you can never add to just the hip area) and angle your side seam in to the original pattern at the waist.

Add practically the same to the hip, and continue to the waist as well as to the hem. This will mean that you have extra fabric at the waist which you can fit in as described above.

Make pattern changes where you need them. This could also apply to the bodice and sleeves.

Fitting for High Hips

Q. I have very sharp hip bones about three inches below my waist. I wasn't aware of this until I began fitting a new skirt of woven fabric. The skirt pulls much too tightly across this area. What should I do?

A. Woven fabrics present a whole new set of fitting problems. However, yours is rather simple to correct. Remember, the fabric you took out of the skirt front in the darts is the amount you will need so the skirt will fit over your high hip bones.

There are two solutions. First, you may eliminate the darts at the front of your skirt completely. Then machine stitch on the exact seamline with a large stitch, pull the bobbin thread and place the excess ease at the spot where the dart was originally; however, even it out so it won't look bunchy. This eliminates the excess fabric and will fit perfectly into the waistband.

The other solution would be to make a curved dart instead of a straight one, using the widest part of the dart at the waistline for fitting. Curve it so that very little fabric is taken away from the skirt at the bone area. Be sure to taper these darts carefully to avoid a pucker of fabric at the end.

Eliminate Back Waistline Bulge

Q. I have had fairly good luck making straight dresses for myself. However, lately I have tried a few with a waistline seam, and they all have a bulge across the waistline in back. Can you suggest an alteration for me to eliminate this excess material?

A. I am sure your problem is the length of the bodice from the shoulder to the waistline. Put on one of these dresses, tie a string very tightly around your actual waistline, place your hands at your waist and be sure the string is in exactly the right spot. You will easily be able to see what your problem is.

If there is excess fabric below the string in the back only, obviously you should shorten the back of your bodice pattern before cutting the garment. In this case, you would have to make the underarm dart deeper in the front so the side seams would come out even. This is commonly done to adjust patterns, especially if you are large in the bust. The deeper dart at the bustline will also achieve a better fitting bodice.

Don't make your dresses too exact, however—allow just a little ease. When you wear a belt, it will draw up the bodice slightly, so I would suggest you allow about ½ inch ease in the bodice length to compensate for the belt.

Too Much Shaping

Q. Everyone thinks I'm so lucky because I have small hips and no tummy. However, I have a very flat derriere, and that is more of a problem than the tummy or hips. No matter how I take a pattern in at the side seams, I still have a wrinkled excess of fabric below the waist and seat. How can I resolve this problem?

A. You share the same figure problem that many of us do. There simply is too much fabric and too much shaping for your body. First, you should take a small fold in your pattern just below the waistline and another small fold down further on the crotch curve. Both folds should be made from the crotch and tapered to nothing at the side seams.

Next, change the darts. The more shape you remove with a dart, the more fabric is added below the dart. I would recommend only one very small dart—the excess width would be folded out in fitting the side seams. I hope these changes will help you.

Some women find that pants without a waistband fit them better, so you might try that also. If you like the contour shaping of the top of the pants, instead of using grosgrain ribbon as a facing, cut the facing the same as your pants pattern. Then attach it in a regular seam at the waist, clip to release the pull of the seam, and machine stitch from the right side about ½ inch below the waist to hold the facing in place. You'll find this a smooth, nice way to finish a skirt, shorts, or slacks.

Sleeves Too Tight

Q. I have never had large arms and never had any difficulty with patterns before. Recently, I noticed they are much tighter than previously. In fact, one dress was practically ruined by not having enough room in the sleeve. Are patterns cut differently today?

A. Pattern measurements are not different today as far as I know. Are you sure you aren't using a pattern marked "for knits only" with woven fabric? Also, if we gain a little weight, it seems to change every part of our body.

My best solution to any of you who have had this problem and aren't sure of the size of the sleeve is, don't cut it out with the rest of the garment. Cut the sleeve out of another piece of fabric, actually baste it into the armhole and check the fit. It could save problems later and only takes minutes to assure a correct fit.

Sleeve Shape

Q. I require more room for my sleeves because of square shoulders and large upper arms. I find that the cap of the sleeves is shaped differently in patterns. Some have a high narrow cap, others a wider, shallow cap. How can I determine the shape of the sleeve before I purchase the pattern?

A. Almost all patterns will have the high, narrow cap sleeve. The exception would be the much more tailored shirt styling where you will find the cap of the sleeve resembling a man's shirt.

If you find a sleeve that fits you well, you can make the sleeves from this pattern on all your garments, provided you also use the armhole from this same pattern.

You will also find that a slightly dropped shoulder will give you more room for your arms and it, too, will be cut with a rather flat sleeve cap.

Armhole Too Tight

Q. I have just finished a sleeveless dress to wear under a jacket. The armhole is so tight in front that it actually leaves red marks. I have never had this problem with dresses that have set-in sleeves. I am narrow in the shoulders—would this make a difference?

A. The clue to the problem is that you are narrow in the shoulders, which would bring the armhole seam out too far for a sleeveless dress. After this, I suggest you take a small fold in your pattern, folding about ¼ inch at the shoulder and tapering to nothing about eight or nine inches below the shoulder. This should bring the armhole to just the right position.

Often this is only necessary in the front, but in your case, it might be necessary in the back as well. If you only need this adjustment in the front, you must also make an adjustment at the back to compensate for the front at the shoulder. Just fold out a small dart in the back of the pattern only. This won't affect the armhole width.

For the garment that is already completed, you may adjust this dress by taking the armhole seam in (front only) a little deeper, tapering from the shoulder to the curve of the armhole. Usually it is not necessary to change the depth of the armhole.

After you have restitched the armhole seam, be sure to clip into the seam allowance to the stitching line to release the pull of the seam. Change a little at a time. It is always possible to restitch a little deeper, but once it is too deep, you have ruined your garment.

Jacket Vent

Q. I recently completed a blazer jacket out of fairly heavyweight double knit. The pattern called for a pleat in the center back of the jacket, but when the jacket was finished, the pleat would not lie flat. What did I do wrong? The jacket was not too tight when it was fitted.

A. Since you didn't give me a pattern number, I can only assume that the pleat should have been constructed like a vent which appears at the back of most blazer jackets.

A vent is left open and is quite different than the construction of a pleat. The top section of the vent is turned back and lies flat over its unturned section. The hems of each side are finished separately.

The only reason I can see that this type of vent would stick out would be in the fitting. Always baste the vent closed before fitting to prevent fitting too tight.

Adding a Yoke

Q. I recently saw a ready-made dress I would like to copy, but it had a contrasting yoke in the front and back, and I can't find a pattern with this same detail. There are many patterns I could use if I knew how to add a yoke. Can you help?

A. Adding a yoke to a pattern is really rather simple. First, decide how far down from the shoulder the yoke would look best. (Usually about four inches from the center of the shoulder would be most flattering.) Carefully mark your pattern and draw a line across it, both front and back, and cut the pattern apart on the line.

The most important part to remember is that you must add your seam allowance to each part of the cut pattern or the bodice will not be long enough. Whenever you cut a pattern apart to add a contrasting color or another detail, always be sure to add the ⅝-inch seam allowance to both parts.

Sport Shirt Shoulder Alteration

Q. I want to make my husband some sport shirts, but have a problem with the neckline. He is stoop-shouldered and the neckline pulls out of shape. What can I do about this?

A. You must alter your husband's pattern before you begin. This adjustment would be the same for a woman that is round-shouldered.

The pattern must be slashed about four inches below the neckline, beginning at the center back and cutting to about one inch from the armhole.

Place another piece of paper under this area and separate the pattern about ½ inch, tapering to nothing at the armhole.

Remark the center back seam, making it straight from the lower part of the shirt to the neckline (you will find the center back is slightly larger at the neckline).

For the neckline to fit the collar, you must take this exact amount out of the neckline in the form of a small dart in your pattern, tapering to nothing about three inches below the neckline.

The extra fabric you have added to the back of the pattern should allow it to fit over the stooped back and still fit the original pattern for the collar.

Straightening Bell Bottoms

Q. I am a novice sewer, but willing to tackle simple tasks. I have some pants that have the bell-bottom shaping at the hem of the legs. I haven't noticed this style being worn anymore. Can I straighten the legs myself rather than taking them to a tailor?

A. Ordinarily, this is a simple alteration that almost anyone can do successfully. Simply turn the pants inside out, take a yardstick and mark a straight line from the knees to the hem—both at the side seams and the inseams—and restitch your seams. If you wish them slightly wider, begin measuring from the hipline where there is slightly more width.

Men's Shirt Alterations

Q. In order to take advantage of sales of men's shirts, I have often had to take a shirt that fits at the neck but is too long in the sleeves. I have tried shortening these sleeves at the caps, but they end up smaller there. To make them fit, I must take the side seams of the shirt in. My next problem is that the tapered shirts don't have any extra to take in at the sides, so I'm lost about this alteration. Can you help me?

A. When you are taking advantage of a sale, you can't always have exactly what you need in the sleeve length.

I still feel that it is much easier to shorten a sleeve at the cap of the sleeve instead of removing the cuffs and cutting the sleeves shorter at the lower end. This also makes the placket too short and in the end, you are doing much more work.

After ripping out the sleeve, carefully measure so you won't cut off too much and make the sleeves too short. Mark the new cutting line with a ruler, and be sure to keep the same curve to the cap of the sleeve. After cutting off the excess fabric, you will notice that the cap of the sleeve is slightly smaller than it was originally. If you can't afford to take in the side seams to offset this, you will have to add a sliver or triangle of fabric to each side of the sleeve at the underarm to extend it to the original size. It will never be noticed since it is at the underarm seam.

From this point on, complete the sleeves as originally stitched.

Shortening Coat Sleeves

Q. My husband has a suit that fits perfectly except for the coat sleeves. They are about an inch too long. What is the best way to shorten them?

A. I only know of one way to shorten the sleeves one inch. First, take out the hem and the lining of the sleeves. Rip as far as necessary to be able to control the fabric without stretching it out of shape, and redo the entire hem to the desired length. The lining will be shortened the same amount.

Do not leave the extra fabric in the garment. A hem that is too wide looks very unprofessional. You must also respace the buttons.

Actually, this isn't too difficult an alteration.

Shorten Shoulder Width

Q. The shoulder seams of all my patterns are too wide. When I shorten the width of the shoulder, do I take the same amount off the top of the sleeves?

A. As a general rule, you would never change the shape of the sleeve cap. This has no bearing on the shoulder width. To make the shoulder width shorter, take a small fold in the pattern, tapering to nothing about six inches below the shoulder. If the shoulder is too wide in back as well as the front, do the same for both front and back. Be sure to make the adjustment on the pattern itself before cutting the garment. This will preserve the correct curve and shape to the armhole.

Zipper Is Too Long

Q. I am just barely five feet tall, so everything is out of proportion for me. My question is this: There is never any mention of choosing your own zipper length depending on your height. When I use the standard twenty-two-inch that is called for on the pattern envelope, I end up sitting on the end of the zipper. Is it all right to substitute a shorter zipper?

A. I'm afraid that patterns are regulated by standards, and from there we must adapt to our own needs. Normally, a zipper should extend seven inches below the waistline. You can measure yourself and decide on the correct length. Probably a twenty-inch zipper would work beautifully for you. Anyone extremely tall might need a twenty-four-inch zipper.

Many pants patterns call for a nine-inch zipper. This again depends on your own figure. If you are small in the waist and large in the hips, you might find a nine-inch zipper is much easier to slip on and off.

Most women choose a seven-inch zipper for skirts and pants, but here again, the choice is up to you. We mustn't take the patterns too seriously. Have the courage to make any changes necessary for yourself.

Alteration for Girls' Patterns

Q. My current problem is sewing for my ten-year-old daughter. The patterns seem to have darts that form too much shape in the bustline, especially for my daughter who hasn't begun to develop yet. She is very self-conscious about the bulge in the fabric that she doesn't fill out. How can I adjust the pattern to her shape?

A. You will adjust your pattern by changing the bustline darts. They should be made about half the depth of the pattern. By making the darts less shaped, you will eliminate the bulge at the bustline.

Often it is possible to eliminate the dart entirely. However, a better fit will be achieved if you retain one of them—just make it smaller. Since most ten-year-olds are fairly straight up and down, you won't have to change the side seams. The front will simply come down slightly longer than the back and this extra fabric can be adjusted when hemming the garment.

Chapter 8
INTERFACINGS

Fusible Webs

There are several fusible webs on the market. All of them come with printed instructions rolled right with the fabric, so save these. Many questions have been asked about fabric shrinking, coming off, and showing through fabric.

A fusible web is used for shaping and is placed between two layers of fabric to be joined. Most of them call for a wet press cloth and pressing with a hot steam iron.

Here is where you will have your first problem. Many fabrics will continue to shrink, even if you have preshrunk them, when pressed again with a wet cloth. This is especially true with knits that contain any wool.

Always pretest the web on the fabric to be used. Fabric shops cannot be responsible for ruined fabric if you didn't follow instructions carefully.

When the two layers of fabric don't stay fused, it's usually because you haven't used enough moisture or enough heat. The webbing can be lifted by pressing with a warm iron and pulling apart. Then, you may re-fuse the fabric with another piece of webbing. If your webbing should come in contact with the sole plate of your iron, remove it immediately with a commercial iron cleaner.

When sewing with lightweight fabrics, again, pretest to be sure you won't have a show-through of the webbing. This product is not recommended for water-repellent fabrics. This finish will prevent the webbing from fusing.

My final advice would be to pretest before application and be sure your fabric has been preshrunk.

Where would you use this type webbing? It's great for finishing the raw edge of a hem. After the hem has been turned up and pressed (or eased, if the skirt is circular), fold the hem back and place a one-inch strip of web ¼ inch below the top of the hem edge and fuse as directed.

It's also good for facings. To secure armhole and neckline facings to the body of a garment, fuse small strips of web at the shoulder and side seams only.

Uses are unlimited—use for patches, appliques, decorator designs, and reversible place mats.

Using Fusible Web

Q. I love the fusible web interfacing, but is there any way to avoid the mess of having it stick to my iron?

A. Yes, it is a mess when it sticks to your iron. I'm sure it has happened to every gal who sews at least once.

I would recommend that whenever you use this web that fuses to two layers of fabric, you cut it slightly smaller than the area to be fused. Carefully place it on the fabric and proceed as the manufacturer's instructions suggest.

Fuse and Fold

Fuse 'n Fold, a Pellon® product, comes packaged and is available in five widths.

Fuse 'n Fold is a strip of fusible interfacing with slots cut out on the foldlines, making it simple to fold over whatever width you need. It produces straight waistbands, plackets, cuffs, and facings of predetermined widths. It isn't necessary to mark or baste in place; just cut to the exact length, place in the correct position and fuse in place.

Fuse 'n Fold can be used on fabrics to be washed as well as dry-cleaned, needs no preshrinking and is compatible with wovens and knits.

If you've had difficulty cutting narrow, straight bands of interfacing, you'll love this precut product. It gives a neat finished banding and certainly saves time.

Interfacing for Lace

Q. I want to make a cotton lace gown but don't know how to finish the seams. Also, do I use interfacing for the front edges and cuffs?

A. If the gown is a shirtwaist style, you may use the featherweight all-bias Pellon® as your interfacing for the collar, cuffs, and front facings. The white showing through is not objectionable.

When you stitch your seams on the regular seam allowance, keep the seams closed and put a second row of stitching about ⅛ inch closer to the cut edges. You may cut the seam allowances off close to the second stitching if you have machine overcasted the seams. It would work fine on lace, but it really isn't necessary. Lace isn't really difficult to work with and is really feminine.

One of my friends has a long shirt dress made of lace, and she wore it originally as a bathing suit cover-up for parties. I was surprised to see her wear it the other night as a formal. She added a long slip-dress to wear under it and a beautiful satin tie belt. It is amazing how much you can really change a garment if you think it out carefully. This is so important today when we want more changes and fewer clothes!

Interfacing for Chiffon

Q. I am making a beautiful chiffon blouse and intend to make more this fall if they are still in style. My problem is, what do I use in the collar, cuffs and front edges for an interfacing? Every kind of interfacing I have tried shows through and spoils the effect of the sheer print.

A. For sheers of any kind, I recommend using organza for the interfacing. This is a firm sheer fabric that will not spoil the effect of the garment, since it is not opaque.

If your garment is a solid color sheer, you might consider using another layer of fabric instead of a separate interfacing. It would only make the color slightly darker and wouldn't change the feeling of the sheer fabric.

When you are making your purchase, check at your shop and experiment with different colors and types until you come up with the right solution.

Interfacing Velvet

Q. I am thinking of making a jacket in velvet for spring. Is spring too late for velvet? However, if I do go ahead, what is the best velvet to buy, what type of interfacing and thread do I use, and most important, how do I press it without making it shiny?

A. I think the velvet you are thinking of is all-cotton. This would be perfect for all climates, all times of the year. The most common type of all-cotton velvet is called velveteen and can be found in printed or solid versions at most fabric shops.

There is a cotton velour which is my favorite, but a little more difficult to find. It has the depth of rayon or silk velvet and is just as luscious. It's very easy to work with versus the rayon velvet.

I would suggest cotton-back velveteen or velvet for any home sewer for best results.

As for thread, either mercerized or polyester thread would be best. As to interfacing, it depends on the type of jacket you are making. You can use the featherweight all-bias Pellon® or a lightweight woven type interfacing that is used in coats and suits.

Pressing is the most difficult of all tasks for the average home sewer. By all means, never touch velvet or velveteen with an iron unless you use a needle board. A needle board is made up of thousands of tiny needles. The velvet is placed face down on the board and then pressed without flattening the pile or nap. If you don't have a needle board, it's best to rely on your dry cleaner for a professional pressing when the garment is completed.

Interfacing for Wool

Q. What is the proper type of interfacing for a wool jacket?

A. You've given me a tough question because there are many answers that could be correct, depending on your ability and the look you want to achieve. If I were making a wool jacket, I would not use a fusible interfacing. Instead, I would use a woven interfacing called ACRO, which is made by the Armo Company. It is flexible and keeps its shape forever.

If you are in a hurry, you might want to use the fusible interfacings. Check the weight, which would depend on the weight of your fabric and the style of the garment.

What Interfacing to Use

Q. There is one thing that leaves me literally stricken when I open up the pattern instructions, and that is the part about interfacings. Patterns differ so much in the technique and are very vague about the type of interfacing that should be used. Can you give me a guideline?

A. The big problem concerning interfacing and the information given on patterns is that they can only give you a general idea since they really have no idea about the fabric you have purchased. They can only help you with the actual fabric they have used for the sample garment.

There are many alternatives in interfacings: the woven versus the unwoven, and the press-on versus the non-press-on. It all depends on the weight and type of your fabric and the type of pattern. Use your own good judgment.

We have had extremely good luck with Pellon®'s dot press-on interfacing. It is very lightweight, only bonds the fabric with tiny pin dots (preventing too much stiffness), and it is so flexible that it has worked with fine matte jerseys as well as heavier fabrics. I hardly think you could make a mistake using this interfacing for most garments, excluding suits and coats where you would need a heavier interfacing. Pellon® also makes a sheer fusible dot.

You might have to experiment with each and every garment by taking a small scrap of fabric and applying several different types of interfacing, finding just the right one for that garment.

In the meantime, try to find a fabric resource center where you can get expert advice on this matter. It can often spell the difference between success and failure.

Press-On Interfacing

Q. I used the press-on interfacing on a blazer jacket of wool knit, and now the fronts of the jacket are at least one inch shorter than the rest of the jacket. I followed the directions carefully. What went wrong?

A. There is one big rule you must remember: Never press the interfacing on the garment itself—just the facings. In your case, the wool knit shrank excessively with the amount of moisture you used. It is always safer to press the interfacings onto the facings or small areas such as top collars, cuffs, and pockets.

Jacket Interfacing

Q. I would like to use fusible interfacing on my jacket as well as on the jacket facing for a crisper look. How can I do this without an outline of the interfacing showing from the right side of the jacket?

A. Ordinarily, I recommend applying the fusible interfacing to the facing of the garment and to the wrong side of your top collar. This is always safe and won't show from the right side. If you wish to apply the fusible interfacing to the garment as well, be sure to cut the outer edge of the interfacing with your pinking shears. This will make an uneven edge and won't be nearly as visible from the right side of the garment.

An extra precaution that I always recommend is to work with a sample of your fabric before deciding on which type of interfacing to use. There are so many available, and the weight of your fabric plus the style of your garment are the deciding factors. With today's softer fashions, you won't be using much stiffening.

Preshrink Woven Interfacing

Q. You advise to preshrink woven interfacing. However, how do you preshrink fusible press-on interfacing without spoiling it?

A. It is not necessary to preshrink fusible interfacing unless it is woven. With woven fusibles, in lightweight or suitweight, simply wet it thoroughly and permit it to dry naturally. Since you won't be pressing it or placing it in the dryer, it will not affect the fusibility.

Shirt Collars

Q. I make men's shirts for my family and would like to know how to stiffen the collars like the ones you purchase. They stay stiff after many washings and don't need to be starched. What do you suggest?

A. There are some types of interfacings that are developed for the manufacturers, and, unfortunately, unavailable for retail sales. We have had very good luck with the lightweight Pellon® dot fusible interfacing, and also a lightweight woven interfacing that is fusible. If it is fused properly, it should remain nice and firm for the life of the garment.

Interfacing Crispness

Q. I am making a long, print shirtwaist dress for my daughter's wedding. I want it to look professional, but am having trouble with the interfacing. Since I'm keeping the dress unlined and wearing a separate slipdress in the background color, the interfacing I have tried for the collar, cuffs and front of the dress shows and looks like a completely different color.

I feel I do need some stiffening for these parts of the garment. What should I use?

A. I would suggest a silk organza. If you can't find silk, a polyester organza would work just as well. Try to find the color that will look most like your print. You will find this will be just enough body for any part of the garment that needs interfacing and will be almost invisible.

Silk organza is also used as an underlining for pure silk garments or any garment that needs just a little more crispness.

Bulky Collars

Q. When I put interfacing into the collar of my garments, the corners become too bulky. When they are turned to the right side, there is an extra bulge at the corners. What am I doing wrong?

A. By allowing the interfacing to come all the way to the corners, there are too many layers of fabric to be turned into such a small space. Before stitching the corners, clip off the interfacing just beyond the stitching line at an angle to the collar points. When the collar is turned, the interfacing will come almost to the end of the collar, but will not appear bulky because it was not included in the seam.

Why Interfacing?

Q. I have just examined a very expensive blouse, and there wasn't a bit of interfacing in the collar or front of the blouse. Why should we use interfacing when this expensive blouse didn't have any?

A. Yes, you will find unusual construction if you look hard enough. It will make you wonder about your own sewing. I usually prefer interfacing of some type, even if you use something as lightweight as silk organza. It helps the inexperienced seamstress make the garment a little more stable.

With very soft fashions, I, too, have noticed that interfacing is occasionally eliminated. I think you will have to use your own good judgment. However, I can't advise you to do without interfacing because in most cases it would be a disaster.

The rule of thumb to remember: Try to consider the style of the garment plus the weight of the fabric before selecting your interfacing. This is the reason we get so confused. If you aren't sure of it, you will have to depend on the advice of a good fabric shop that you have confidence in. Usually, there is more than one choice of interfacing for all garments. Don't be tempted to use the wrong thing just because you have some left over.

Chapter 9
LINING AND UNDERLINING

With the importance of knits in the home sewing picture, we aren't using underlining as much as we did with woven fabrics. Underlining means basting a second piece of lightweight fabric to the wrong side of your garment fabric for extra body, either because of the design of the pattern or the weight of the fabric. From that point on, you would forget that there were two pieces of fabric and you would treat them as one.

Knits are never underlined because you would lose the stretch factor of the knit fabric. When it is desirable to line knits, they are separately lined. Purchase a piece of lightweight fabric such as china silk for garments to be dry-cleaned, or polyester that resembles china silk for washable garments.

This makes a beautiful separate, free-hanging lining that is attached to the neckline, waistline, zipper, and is usually free at the hem. I have seen garments that are separately lined with the lining lightly tacked to the hemline of the garment. This gives the garment a beautifully finished appearance.

There is one cardinal rule to remember: If the garment is to be washed, any underlining or lining should be preshrunk to prevent its shrinking more than the garment fabric. Otherwise, the result would be a puckered look.

For those of you who began your sewing with knits, you are going to find a completely new world of sewing when you work with woven fabrics, which are returning with great importance. Underlining will be one of the techniques you will have to master for perfect results in a shaped garment.

Using Underlining Less

Q. So many patterns don't suggest any kind of underlining today. Why is that?

A. Underlining was used extensively when we wore very straight skirts and dresses. It not only kept the line of the design from changing, due to the extra body it gave the fabric, but it also prevented the fabric from sitting out in the back.

If you choose a pattern with these same lines today (and they are coming back), you would still use a lightweight underlining. Treat the two layers of fabric as one and·proceed with your construction.

With the many knits on the market today—matte jerseys, double knits, interlock knits—the patterns have much more ease and fullness. Therefore, any underlining would destroy the design of the pattern. For these types of garments, there are only a few areas where any type of interfacing is used.

For see-through knits, or where you are afraid the knit will cling to the body more than you desire, you will need to make a separate slip-type lining, connected at the shoulder, or else completely free hanging as a slip.

Lining Slacks

Q. How do you feel about lining slacks? I try to find the double knits that are not see-through, but it is more and more difficult.

A. I really am not in favor of lining double knit washable polyester slacks. I have examined some of the better slacks, and often there is a lining that extends to the hipline; however, these are not usually washable. I would suggest searching thoroughly for the opaque double knits in solid colors.

If you are making silk or fibranne pants, or anything that would be dry-cleaned, you may underline or separately line these. Be sure your underlining has been preshrunk, even with garments that will be dry-cleaned.

I have had a session with my dry cleaner about the disasters that come up from cleaning, usually not the fault of the cleaner. However. they are blamed for these often costly mishaps.

First, remove your buttons—most of them could be ruined in some cleaning solvents. Next, pin a scrap of your leftover fabric onto the garment to be cleaned. In this way, they can examine it thoroughly and if there is any doubt as to how it will come out, they will run the sample fabric through first.

If you have used quality underlinings as well as quality fabric, you should have excellent results with dry cleaning. For your better clothes that aren't worn often, garments can remain new for several seasons, much longer than if they were washed at home. I am not referring to wash and wear fabrics for everyday wear—just those specials that you have spent many hours making and want to keep very nice.

Silk Dress

Q. How would I go about lining a silk dress, and what type of sewing machine needle should I use?

A. The procedure for lining a silk dress would depend on your pattern. If it is extremely straight, you'll want to underline the entire dress.

When you baste the underlining and the dress fabric together, be sure not to pull either of them too tight; then treat them as if they were only one piece of fabric. This will greatly reinforce the seams and keep the silk from pulling away at the points of stress.

If the dress is loose-fitting, you may add a separate lining. For elegance you could use china silk, but because of the cost, you might prefer to line the dress in any lightweight, woven polyester that resembles china silk.

Since silk is a delicate woven fabric, use a regular machine needle, size 9 or 11. NEVER use a ball-point needle for woven fabrics.

Silk

Q. I have just discovered a raw silk dress in the designer salon for over $300. It didn't have one inch of lining in it. You have always suggested underlining these fabrics. For this price, wouldn't you have expected to find a lining?

A. This is a matter of personal preference and how much wear you are going to give the dress. I imagine that any woman who spends over $300 for a simple dress won't wear it as a uniform. It's possible also that the style of the dress required the softness of an unconstructed fabric.

If you expect to wear a dress often, I think you will be more satisfied underlining it with very lightweight fabric. This is especially true with a fabric such as the hand-loomed India pure silks which are rather fragile.

Also, unless you are pencil slim, you will find the garment will hold its shape if it is underlined. Without it, the seams are almost certain to pull the fabric at any point where there is the least amount of stress.

Many of the beautiful oriental silks are separately lined with a lightweight china silk. You could also use a very lightweight polyester lining that resembles silk. This lining is attached to the neckline, armholes, zipper, and covers the hem, hiding all the construction of the garment and making it easier to slip on and off. This also affords extra body to the silk and keeps the original shape intact.

Woven Cottons

Q. I'm afraid I have fallen into the habit of working with knits for so long that I simply don't know how to treat woven cottons. Should they be lined or not?

A. These cottons you are referring to are usually the semi-fitted shift-type patterns that look perfect if they aren't overfitted. The lining keeps the shape of the dresses, since the dresses are usually trimmed heavily in heavy cotton lace.

The kind of fabric and the type of pattern are the factors in determining whether or not a garment is to be lined. The more fullness or softness in the pattern, the less lining or construction you would use.

Usually, the length of a dress could also determine the construction. Unless you are talking about a sheer fabric that would lose its effect if it were underlined, I would underline most other fabrics because they will hang better and not appear limp because of the added length.

Chiffon Blouse

Q. I bought some of the printed chiffon fabric for a blouse just like the ready-made blouses. Now I have lost my courage. The ready-made blouses aren't lined, but I feel mine should be. What would I line it with so I wouldn't lose the effect and still make my blouse a little more opaque?

A. Lining these sheer blouses often depends on the color of the background of the print. Some are more opaque than others. Hold the fabric up to yourself, over your bra or slip, and then decide if it is necessary to line.

To keep the blouse washable, you must also use washable lining of the same texture. My suggestion would be to line it with polyester chiffon, which comes in all colors. You should experiment with the colors that might look best under your print.

Usually a flesh color is best since you probably won't line the sleeves. Treat the two pieces of fabric as one. In other words, you'll be underlining the sections you want more opaque. (See figure 9.)

Fig. 9 – Lining a Chiffon Blouse

Some of the very expensive chiffons I have seen are made of several layers of chiffon, varying in color. They are truly beautiful, but, because of the fabric, are never easy to work with. Polyester chiffon has the weight of georgette and isn't as slippery as the old silk chiffons. Therefore, it's much easier to work with and is much less expensive.

Corduroy

Q. Is it necessary to line a coat made out of corduroy? I want to keep it casual. Yet, if I don't line it, the little globs of the nap get on all my clothes and are difficult to brush off. What should I do?

A. There are ways of finishing seams of corduroy to avoid these little tufts continuously coming off as you wear the garment. You really shouldn't leave seams with cut edges.

If you prefer the jacket unlined, cut your seams slightly wider than ⅝ inch so you will have enough room to turn the edges over about ⅛ inch and topstitch close to the edge. You may also bind the seams.

You may also make a flat-felled seam. This finish is used quite often commercially. This is done by trimming one side of the seam allowance close to the machine stitching of the seam. Fold the extended edge over the shorter seam allowance, turning the edge in and machine stitching about ¼ inch from the seam.

Lastly, I suggest a very lightweight polyester lining. It is almost easier to apply a lining than to finish all the seams of your jacket and it will not add bulk. It will slide over sweaters and shirts much better.

Lightweight Knit

Q. I am a large woman and have selected a pattern for knits only. Since the knit I will be using is not very heavy, I think I should line this dress. What kind of lining should I use?

A. This is a question that comes up very often, whether you are large or not. First, never underline a knit. This would destroy the give of the knit, and the garment wouldn't hang or fit the way it should.

If you wish to line a knit dress, use a free-hanging lining. This could be made of a tricot fabric or a polyester lining that resembles china silk. Be sure it is attached at the neckline only. You may finish the edges at the zipper by slip stitching loosely to this area. Finish the hem of the lining separately from the hem of the dress.

You will find that most of the knits in ready-to-wear have absolutely no lining. Therefore, it might be a good idea to purchase a little heavier knit for your dress. The very lightweight knits and jerseys are shown in fuller dresses with gathers and a flared skirt.

Linings in Winter Coats

Q. I happen to live in an area where winters are very severe, and I want to make a warm winter coat. Therefore, I need help on the lining. Why are all coats lined with silk-type fabric? This causes static electricity, and besides, it's plain cold. Is it possible to line a coat with fake fur?

A. It is not only possible, but practical and in high fashion as well, to line a coat in fake fur. Going to the other extreme, there are poplin coats available that are lined in mink and other precious furs, so don't be afraid to copy the idea.

The most important step before beginning is the selection of your pattern. You must check the lines of the coat to be sure there will be enough room for a more bulky lining.

You can usually see by the sketch on the pattern envelope if the coat or jacket is to be worn over a lightweight blouse or dress, or if it looks like a garment to be worn over sweaters and jackets. I also recommend that you try to find a pattern with drop shoulders or raglan sleeves—the bulky fur cloth will be much easier to apply.

There are many fake furs that would be lovely in a coat. Try not to get ones that are too thick and bulky since they will all have about the same warmth. Apply the way you would any lining; however, a pleat in back isn't necessary. Baste in your garment before you complete the lining to be sure you haven't pulled it too tight.

Another successful lining for coats would be a lightweight knit. It adds warmth without too much bulk. The reason coats are usually lined with silk-type linings is that they slide on and off much easier than knit or fur linings. Because everyone's comfort is different, select what is best for you. Don't be afraid to try something new.

Straight Skirts

Q. I'm so glad to see the long straight skirts coming back. I always loved those deep slits that we used to have a few years ago. My problem is that when you do use a deep slit, the skirt looks unfinished on the inside. Is it necessary to underline this type of skirt or will a separate slip do?

A. A separate slip will never do because the slit in the slip will not come to the exact place as the slit in the skirt. You should underline your skirt; then finish the hem and the facing edges with hem lace. Now if the slit separates, as it surely will, it will look almost as attractive on the wrong side as on the right side. You will find more and more of these slits in straight skirts. You may use the slit at the center front, side or center back, whichever you prefer.

How to Add Jacket Lining

Q. Why do so many of the new patterns for jackets eliminate the linings? I hate to put on a wool jacket and have it stick to a dress or sweater. What is the best way to add a lining when there is not a pattern for one?

A. These jackets and blazers you see today without the linings are all part of the softer, more unconstructed type of clothing being worn. I am with you on this—I don't like jackets without a lining either. You can add a very lightweight lining out of woven polyester that resembles china silk and have no more bulk or weight to your jacket.

If there is no pattern for the lining, place the jacket facing over the jacket front pattern. Add 1¼ inches extra to the remaining front section of pattern. This will be absorbed by the seam allowance of the facing and the lining.

When cutting the lining for the back of the jacket, if it is fitted, you will need about two inches extra at the center back for a pleat in the lining. This will give you extra comfort and is usually necessary for woven-type fabrics. The sleeves can be cut the same as the jacket sleeves.

It's good to remember not to fit the lining too tightly. It should always be a little looser than the garment fabric. Allow a little extra fold at the hem of the jacket lining and the sleeve lining for additional ease.

I have always found it almost simpler to add a lining than it is to finish all the seams nicely, as you would have to do with an unlined garment.

Chapter 10
PATTERN DETAILS

Shawl Collars

Q. I am confused about shawl collars that I have seen in fashion articles. How are they constructed?

A. It's good to be aware of the ready-to-wear fashion scene before choosing your own patterns. The shawl collar suits are new.

A shawl collar is one that has slightly different construction. The facing continues to form the top collar. There is no notch or seam in the collar such as we find in the classic notched collar jackets. Otherwise, this jacket looks very similar to the blazer jackets we have seen.

Full-Length from Short Pattern

Q. Do you have any advice for making a long dress from a pattern for a short one? Can any pattern be made long or short?

A. Many patterns are interchangeable, and there are also many patterns in the books that show both lengths for your choice. If you like the lines of your short dress, I see no reason why it can't be made full-length. Many styles change from morning to evening wear simply by using a different fabric.

The simplest way to change to the longer length is to have someone measure you from the center back at your neckline down to the desired length.

Next, check the length of the garment given on your pattern. You will add the difference. Take a yardstick and simply extend the side seams to your new length, using the same angle, which will make your skirt much wider at the hemline. This is necessary to give you room to walk or dance.

Sleeveless Blouse

Q. My favorite blouse pattern fits me perfectly and I can make it without checking and rechecking the pattern instructions. I would love to use this pattern for a sleeveless blouse, but the pattern calls for sleeves. Can I still use this pattern and cut my own facings?

A. There is a slight change you must make before cutting your blouse. The armholes on a sleeveless garment must be cut higher than on one with sleeves.

Place another piece of paper under your pattern at the underarm area. Cut the armhole at least ½ to ⅝ inch higher, curving up to nothing at the notches in front and back. Also, you will probably find that the blouse should be taken in at the side seams about ½ inch to make the armhole smaller.

After fitting the garment to be sure the armhole is fitting properly, you may cut the armhole facing from the new pattern and apply it as you would any facing. Be sure to clip the seam allowance at the underarm curves after stitching the facing to the garment. This will release the fabric, and the result will be a nice smooth facing with no pulling areas.

One last tip would be to understitch the facing. This means to bring all the seams toward the facing and machine stitch close to the seam on the facing itself. This stitching will prevent the facing from slipping out and showing the right side. Don't stitch the entire facing to the armhole. The indentation will show and make the garment look homemade. For a professional finish, simply tack the facing at the shoulder and underarm seams.

Interchangeable Skirts

Q. I just love everything about my new suit pattern with the exception of the bias skirt. Could I use the same pattern and simply change the skirt?

A. Yes, skirts are interchangeable if you find a skirt that has approximately the same style lines to go with the rest of the pattern. If a bias skirt isn't flattering to you, choose another pattern as a substitute. However, try to choose a pattern that has the same width at the hemline and one that will look equally well with the lines of the rest of your pattern. This is one of the extra bonuses that we home sewers have over those who must wear whatever the manufacturer decides.

Spaghetti Straps

Q. What is the best advice you can give us on making spaghetti straps?

A. With woven fabrics, these straps should be cut on the bias. I also prefer using a small string as an insert. It keeps the straps nice, firm, and rounded.

Cut a bias strip of fabric about one inch wide. The small string or cording to be used inside should be cut twice the length of the finished strip. Fold the string in half and fasten the halfway point to the end of your bias strip on the right side of the fabric.

Next, fold the bias strip in half over the string, right sides together. Begin machine stitching about ⅛ to ¼ inch from the fold, encasing the string and pulling the fabric slightly as you stitch. When the stitching is completed, cut the excess fabric from your folded strip. You should have exactly the same amount of fabric on both sides of the stitching line.

Now you are ready to turn the strip right side out. Gently pull the string that is extending at the end. The beginning is the most difficult part, and you have to gently coax it through. Once it has begun to turn in, you will have no further problem. Keep the bias in one position. Don't allow it to twist as you turn it right side out.

If you have done this correctly, you should have a nice, tight, cording that looks very professional. (See figure 10.)

Fig. 10 – Spaghetti Straps

Longer Neck Placket

Q. A pattern I recently completed has a short placket closing at the front neckline. If I make the dress again, would it spoil the design to make this placket longer and add an additional button?

A. For those of us who are used to having a larger opening in our dresses and shirts, this can be very frustrating. Examine the style of your dress pattern before you change this detail. It might not look right if you add another button.

There is another solution, however. You may add a seam allowance to the center back of your dress if there isn't a seam in the pattern. I would add about ¾ inch while you are at it. Insert a regular lapped zipper. If the closing involves the collar, you may also add a seam to the center back of the collar.

Your garment will look exactly like the pattern from the front, but because of the zipper closing you have added, it will be much easier to slip on and off. The measurements will remain the same. Please try it—it works!

Knit Binding

Q. I have been making some simple T-shirts for summer. They have turned out very well and I am excited about beginning something more difficult. One of the shirts in the pattern shows a binding of a contrasting color. Is it necessary to cut this binding on the bias?

A. With stretch knits, the binding strips should not be cut on the bias. The cross-stretch of the fabric has all the give you will need.

When working with woven fabrics with no stretch, any binding must be cut on the bias so it will have the proper give for the curves.

Instructions vary completely from woven fabrics to stretch fabrics. It's best to learn how to handle both.

Correcting Blouson Bodice

Q. I have just completed my latest disaster. It was beautiful in the picture, but on me, it is horrendous. My pattern had a blouson bodice. It is much too full, stiff, and downright unflattering. Since the elastic was threaded through a casing, I think it can be salvaged. How should I begin?

A. Blouson bodices or jackets are tricky things. They can look great, or be placed in the wrong position and turn into a disaster. It's a simple matter to adjust before applying the casing to your pattern.

The problem is the length of your waistline from the shoulder, and also your body proportions. Usually, a blouson effect requires a very slender body. If you are a little lumpy in the midsection, it has a tendency to make you look thicker through the waist.

Before you begin with the casing, try the bodice on. Take a string and tie it tightly around your waist; then ease up the fabric to whatever point is becoming to your own figure. When the ease is adjusted perfectly for your figure and the weight of the fabric (remember, a stiff fabric will not give you that soft drapable effect), carefully mark under the pins in six or eight places from front to back. Remove the bodice and make the pins even to make an accurate place for your casing.

This adjustment takes only minutes. It saves having to toss out something you have completed. We must all save ourselves from these disappointments if we are going to love sewing.

Fig. 11 – Trimming a Shirt

Trimming a Shirt

Q. I have seen many tailored shirts of cotton plaids, stripes and men's wear fabrics that have an edging of lace around the collars, cuffs and front bands. Is it possible to add lace to ready-made shirts for this new look? If so, what type would I purchase?

A. This little touch started with the top designers and has continued. (See figure 11.)

Yes, you may add lace to a ready-made shirt. Try to find a narrow val-type lace (usually polyester) that is already gathered onto a very narrow band of netting. The entire width is only a little over ½ inch, so you will have only a tiny edge peeking over the edges. Hand whip this lace trim on the wrong side of your collar, cuffs and, if possible, to each side of the front band of the shirt.

If you can't find lace pregathered on the tiny band, you might have to gather it yourself. This, however, is a little more tedious to apply.

Chapter 11
SKIRTS

Economical Skirts

Q. I recently moved from a small town to a large city, and I'm aghast at the prices of better ready-to-wear garments. What could possibly make a wool skirt cost $100?

A. Most skirts that retail for around $100 cost the manufacturer less than $15 for the fabric. The rest of the cost depends on the designer's name and the number of garments produced.

If you purchase a good quality wool (from $10 to $15 per yard), the finest skirt you could make would cost less than $30. This shows how, by sewing, you can have the joy of wearing the loveliest of fabrics for less money than it would take to purchase the cheapest ready-mades.

Advantages of Bias Cut

Q. What is the advantage of a bias cut skirt if you are using a solid color?

A. When a garment is cut on the bias, it molds closer to the body and eliminates added bulk. This applies to skirts, coats, and jackets. Pauline Trigere, the world famous designer, was probably the original designer of bias cuts. Her clothes are still cut with the beautiful bias lines. They retail for thousands of dollars.

Today, Calvin Klein has used the bias cut for his dirndl skirt pattern, and I must say that it fits beautifully. Somehow the gathers for the skirt are not as bulky. It is usually possible to cut almost any pattern without pleats on the bias. You might do a little experimenting yourself since skirts are important to everyone's wardrobe.

Long Bias Skirts

Q. I don't need very dressy holiday clothes, but I would like to make a long skirt to wear with my blouses and blazers. Can you give suggestions?

A. I like bias skirt patterns, which can be found in any catalogue.

Be sure to check the measurements on the pattern envelope and compare them to yours; then add the difference at the side seams. Never measure the actual pattern pieces as you may forget to add the ease for proper fitting.

I cut the side seams slightly wider than necessary, usually about two to three inches overall. This is added at the waist and tapered to nothing slightly below the hips. I then stitch two rows of machine stitching at the waist and pull up the ease slightly.

I apply the zipper to the side seam, and allow the skirt to hang a day or so before hemming.

Having Trouble with Bias

Q. I am having trouble with the bias skirts. The one I prefer has a center front and back seam; therefore, it has a little more fullness than appeals to me. My problem is that the skirt seams flare out at the hem instead of hanging evenly and straight. The hems also seem too full and bunchy. Can you give us some tips since most of us sew these skirts?

A. There are several points to remember about working with bias seams. First, always add at least one extra inch to the seam allowance when cutting. Bias seams will be smoother if they have the extra width, rather than the skinny seam allowance that tends to twist.

Besides, since you must allow the skirt to hang for a few days before seaming, you will find you need more width than you expected because the fabric will pull narrower and longer.

Most women have a tendency to ease in bias seams as they stitch, but this is wrong. You must stretch the bias seams as you stitch them. This gives you the proper hang to your seams and will avoid that drawn-up look, as well as popped seams. If a seam hasn't been stretched, the stitches will crack and break as you wear your garment.

As for extra fullness at the hemline, first remember that bias hems should be narrow, possibly no wider than one inch. This will take out most of the excess fabric.

It could be that you must make your seamline a little deeper from the foldine of the hem to the cut edge. Angle the seam in a little; this will remove the extra bulk.

The most important point to remember is not to stretch it as you press. Again, I can't stress caution too much.

Don't use long ironing strokes. Instead, simply press the iron up and down, always easing the fabric slightly, never allowing it to stretch.

Last, but not least, don't blame your dry cleaner if the hem comes back slightly uneven. This is the nature of the cut of the fabric and often cannot be avoided. As with most assets, there are liabilities, and this is one you will have to cope with if you want the beautiful look of bias.

Lining Bias Skirts

Q. Would you give us some tips on linings for the bias skirts?

A. First, if a bias skirt needs to be underlined, cut the underlining on the bias also. If the bias skirt is extremely full (not an A-line), I would not recommend underlining at all. Instead, you may add a separate, free-hanging lining attached to the waistline and the zipper area only.

Be sure to allow your bias skirts to hang for several days before hemming. No matter how much care you take, they will continue to grow or stretch as long as you keep them hanging on a hanger.

The next important point to remember is not to fit the waistline and hips too tight. The bias will allow the fabric to stretch. If the skirt is fit too tight, you will have a skirt that will pull in again under the hips and will never hang evenly and freely.

Be sure to make the skirt larger than your own waistline, put in two rows of gathering stitches at the waistline, and pull the threads slightly, easing the top of the skirt. Then attach this to your waistband. This extra ease, if done carefully, will not look gathered. Instead, it will fit nicely over your hips and avoid pulling.

A last word of advice—if you have a large tummy or large rounded hips (please be honest with yourself), avoid this bias skirt altogether. You can find many fabrics that are printed or woven in a design that looks as if it were cut on the bias. Make your skirt from these fabrics and it will be much more attractive.

Zippers for Bias Skirts

Q. How can I sew the zipper of a bias skirt without its wrinkling?

A. There is no easy way to apply a zipper in a bias skirt without rippling, so I recommend you apply it to a side seam rather than the center back or front. Be sure not to pull the fabric too taut because it is cut on the bias, but the tape of the zipper is cut on the straight grain. I would carefully take the time to baste in the zipper before machine stitching. This way, you can try the skirt on before the final stitching.

Another problem could be in the fitting—too often we depend on the stretch of the fabric to give us extra allowance. However, you must always ease a bias skirt onto the waistband to avoid the pulled look.

Golf Skirts with Attached Shorts

Q. How do you go about attaching shorts to a skirt pattern?

A. Not being a golfer, I had to check these out. Surprisingly enough, some of the ready-made skirts with pants attached were around $40. All I could think of was how much you could save by making this garment.

Most of the skirts are made from simple A-line patterns, often slit at the hem for extra ease and freedom. Naturally, they are very short, and therefore, the pants become part of the ensemble.

Baste the shorts to the unfinished waistline of the skirt and enclose the raw edges together with the skirt when applying the skirt band. You simply leave seven inches open at the center back, hemming the raw edges. The zipper will only be in the skirt; the opening for the shorts will hang free from the skirt.

For a neat finish, add a band about three inches wide to the hem of the shorts to match the skirt fabric. If you have used other types of trims, these could be added to the shorts instead. Use your own imagination for fabric, color, and trim.

Pleat Problems

Q. Whenever I use pleats in a skirt, even if I only use one at the center front, the skirt seems to hang longer at this point and the pleat often gapes open instead of hanging smooth and sharp. Should a pleat have special instructions in addition to those given on the pattern?

A. The weight of the extra fabric involved in pleats often tends to make them hang longer. You can avoid this, as well as the droopiness of the area where the pleats are involved.

Instead of using the ⅝-inch seamline for the skirt at the area of the pleats, try bringing the skirt up a little higher, possible ¼ to ½ inch deeper than the seamline, and then gradually go back to the ⅝-inch seam allowance. This will take care of the extra weight of the pleat.

Since every fabric produces a different weight, try on your skirt before deciding how much to lift it at the pleat area.

Pleats look sharper if you stitch the inside fold of the pleat through the hem. From the inside of the skirt, fold on the pressed inside fold, machine stitch through all thicknesses of the hem, beginning at the edge of the hem and stitching toward the top of your skirt. This stitching is done about ⅛ to ¼ inch from the fold, and is only necessary through the hem. It keeps the pleat from gaping open.

Knits and Pleats

Q. Will knit fabric pleat well?

A. Pleats naturally suggest crispness; therefore, a woven hard-finished fabric would pleat most successfully. If the pleats can look like unpressed folds instead of razor sharp creases, you could use your knit fabric. I have seen pleats stitched on the very edge in knits, just as pants are often stitched at the creases.

As a rule, remember that soft, clingy, or napped fabrics will not pleat well. Therefore, it would be much better to make your skirt with gores or a bias cut for that flippy look.

Center Front Pleats

Q. My latest skirt has a center front pleat which was made with a separate underlay section. I simply can't seem to press this pleat nice and smooth—it wants to pop out. In my opinion, it looks very homemade. What can I do?

A. When there is a seam within the pleat, it is much easier to solve this problem than where there is no seam. When stitching the underlay to the skirt fronts, end your stitching about eight inches above the hemline.

Next, have the length of the skirt marked for the correct length, and actually complete the hem. The front sections will be hemmed in three separate sections. After the hem is completed, you are ready to finish the seams.

Pin the underlay to the fronts and machine stitch through the hem up to the point where your stitching ended (always begin at the hem and work up). These seams should not be pressed open. Overcast the seams if they tend to ravel. At the lower edge of the hem, you may wish to turn under the corner of the raw edges at an angle and whip to the hem by hand.

This method of stitching the seams within a pleat will guarantee a nice, flat finished hem.

Skirts with Stripes

Q. I love horizontally striped fabric, but each time I use it, I have the same problem with the hem. If the skirt is A-line and I have someone mark my hem even with the floor, the stripes are never even at the hemline. What would you suggest?

A. The only skirts that are really straight at the hemline would be the kind that are made with a straight piece of fabric, gathered or pleated in at the waistline without any further shaping. All other skirts will be slightly uneven at the hemline as you will notice when cutting.

If you have your skirt measured evenly with a hem marker, the hem will also curve slightly. The more A-line the skirt, the more the hem will curve.

I think each piece of fabric should be examined individually, and then you should decide which is more important, the stripe or the hemline.

If the stripe is not only bold, but wide as well, you can often place it when cutting so that if the hemline is slightly curved, it will be within the stripes and hardly be noticed when wearing. If the stripes are more of the shadow kind, it really won't be noticed one way or the other.

This is one point that you must decide on individually. After all, it's the overall picture that is important. These little points of controversy are only important as you are working on the construction. Don't take them too seriously—just see that the end results are attractive.

Waistbands Are Tricky to Fit

Q. When should a skirt be fitted? Before or after applying the waistband?

A. The skirt must be fitted separately, just as the waistband must be fitted before the two can be attached. I have always suggested stitching a row of machine stitching with the longest stitch on the seamline of the skirt. Ease up the stitching slightly, especially on each side of the side seams, front and back. If you have a large tummy, ease slightly over the stomach area and eliminate front darts.

Try the skirt on to see if it fits nicely over the curves of your body. Be sure it isn't too tight. If it is, it will form a fold of fabric just below the waistband and look very unattractive.

Next, fit the waistband to yourself, marking the spot where it will overlap. The extension of your waistband should be on the underside; the top side of the waistband should end at the zipper. Now, carefully pin the waistband over the eased skirt—remember, the skirt must always be slightly larger than the waistband.

Try your skirt on. If it fits perfectly, you are ready to machine stitch the waistband. Be sure to pin it frequently to prevent slipping, but remember to remove the pins before stitching over them.

These same instructions will apply to pants as well as skirts.

Hemming Circular Skirts

Q. What is the secret to hemming a circular skirt?

A. Use a narrow hem. You can ease excess fabric in a wider hem if it is wool, and it shrinks in. However, many fabrics today will not shrink, so I never advise using a wide hem.

If the fabric is cotton, I would simply turn up the hem, machine stitch on the edge about ½ inch above the first stitching and cut off the excess.

Remember, a bias edge will not ravel, so never use lace or seam tape to finish a bias hem.

Waistband Problem

Q. My waistband is the same size as the skirt and it gapes in back. Since my fabric is brocade, it doesn't seem to be strong enough to rip. How can I make the waistband fit better?

A. First, the waistband should be fitted to your body before you apply it to the skirt. The top of the skirt should be at least two inches larger than the waistband and gradually eased to the waistband. You may have to ease more if you are using a woven fabric and your figure juts out suddenly below the waistline.

This ease you have used allows the skirt or pants to follow the body contours and not ride up, causing folds of fabric to form just below the waistband.

As to your immediate problem, I would suggest making a casing of your waistband and inserting elastic to the back area only. This will hold the excess fabric close to your body and shouldn't add too much bulk. The elastic can be attached to the waistband on the inside at each of the side seams.

Elastic Waistbands for Skirts

Q. How can I put an elastic waistband in a skirt?

A. It is very simple to apply elastic to a skirt instead of a conventional waistband, providing that the fabric is suitable. Your fabric should be lightweight and soft to avoid excess bulk. Also, be sure you really want elastic.

Most knit pants are constructed with elastic waistbands because women usually wear overblouses or sweaters with them. If you wear a tuck-in blouse with a skirt, you might not like the gathers and excess bulkiness.

To make an elastic waistband on your skirt, eliminate the darts at the waist, add at least an inch in length for the turnover of your casing, and insert nonroll elastic in the casing.

Try your skirt on after you have arranged the ease evenly and see if it fits the way you want. You may want to adjust the ease to flatter your body.

After the ease is adjusted, sew vertically through the elastic and the casing in four evenly spaced spots to keep the ease where you want it and to keep the elastic from rolling over.

Full Skirts

Q. With the fullness in most of the skirts today, how can we judge how full a skirt really is by the pattern sketch?

A. You must look on the pattern envelope, and most of them will tell you the width at the hemline. If the skirt is fifty-four inches wide at the hem, this is about as narrow as you can get your skirt and your skirt won't look huge. Some skirts will be over 100 inches at the hem. See the difference?

Also, if the skirt is cut on the bias, the width isn't as important because it will hang closer to your body and won't seem as bulky as one cut on the straight of the fabric.

You can adjust the gathers at the waistband so that they are most flattering to you. If your tummy is quite large, avoid gathers across the front. You also can reduce the excess fabric at the waist by taking small darts every five or six inches. Make them about ¼ to ½ inch deep at the waist and taper them to nothing about six inches below the waist. The darts will be hidden in the gathers and won't really show. They will just eliminate some of the fullness where you might not want it.

Gathered skirts do take a little getting used to—the first time you wear them, you will feel very fat. However, for summer they are so comfortable; and when you see everyone else in them, you, too, will begin to like this look. So, choose a pattern that is just full enough for your body. You can really save money making skirts. They are so unreasonably expensive in ready-to-wear.

Waistband Width

Q. Is there a correct width for the waistband of a skirt?

A. The width of the waistband depends partly on your body—the more flesh you have at the waistline, the more difficulty you will have. First, be sure to use press-on interfacing for the waistband or a nonroll belting.

I prefer waistbands no wider than about ¾ inch. This makes a very neat band and will seldom double over. It is also possible to make your skirt without a waistband. Either cut a facing the same size and shape as the top of the skirt, or use a grosgrain ribbon inside the skirt instead of a waistband.

There are actually contour skirts that are faced, and these work beautifully.

If you are cutting a waistband out of your fabric, try to use the selvage edge for one edge of the waistband. This will avoid the bulk of having to turn in both edges and, because the fabric is more firmly woven on the selvage, it helps keep the waistband from stretching.

When applying the waistband to your skirt, keep the front end even with the folded edge of the zipper. Be sure, however, to allow at least two inches extra for the under side to lap. Use the large, flat skirt hooks for a smooth waistband as well as a sturdy one.

If you apply the new "Waist-Shaper," a fusible interfacing, you may use a 1-1/4-inch or two-inch waistband. The interfacing will keep the waistband nice and firm.

Can You Save Yardage?

Q. With the tiny hems used on most of the fuller skirts, isn't it possible to save on yardage if your pattern had the conventional amount of width for the hem?

A. The amount of fabric you must purchase depends on the actual layout of the pattern, and the length of the finished garment versus the length of your actual garment. Since skirts are being worn slightly longer, it will often be very important to check the finished length of the pattern on your envelope; then decide whether you need more or less fabric.

Some of us keep patterns for years, especially a favorite skirt pattern. You may actually need to lengthen this old pattern five or six inches. Check carefully before deciding to cut down on the amount of fabric for any garment. I find that unless the width of the fabric is different than the pattern states, there is very little fabric left over.

Chapter 12
PANTS

Proper Fitting Pants

The proper assembly of slacks is very important for a successful appearance. It's amazing what the wrong sequence of assembly can produce.

First, sew the inseams of each leg and press. Then sew the side seams of each leg. Before the two legs are joined, press the creases permanently.

Next, pin the crotch seams and stitch from the center back through the inseam and continue to the front. You might also double stitch the places of greatest strain.

Using this procedure will assure your slacks of hanging beautifully and correctly without that unattractive U curve at the crotch.

It takes more than fitting to make pants look great—it takes a great figure. Unfortunately, all female figures were not made to wear pants, so if you are honest with yourself and realize this is your problem, you must attack the problem from another angle.

Of course, the fitting is important. You must use the right width legs for your figure, the crotch length must be correct and the pants must fit with some ease throughout the thigh and hip area. After you have achieved a satisfactory fit, then we must find what will make these pants attractive on you. This will come from the type of top or jacket you wear with the pants to disguise the part of your figure that is not attractive.

An overblouse or shirt is the first answer that comes to my mind. A shirt-type or blazer jacket will also hide a multitude of sins.

Whatever you do, I would avoid a tuck-in blouse or even a short sweater that reveals the very part of you that you are trying to disguise. I hope I have given you a few ideas that will overcome the hurdle you have encountered and allow you to wear slacks with confidence, just the same as your friends.

We all need to spend time examining our own figures to see just what pattern lines will enhance it the most and also what pattern lines to avoid. This applies to all types of garments, not only slacks.

Best Pants Pattern for You

Q. Slacks seem to be going back to the trouser look with the pleats just below the waistband. Won't this be a much more difficult pant to wear than the ones with darts?

A. The kind of pants pattern we select has always been determined by our figures, no matter what they show in magazines. You must decide what's best for you.

Yes, the more masculine trouser pant is the newest look in pants because of the very tailored flannel suits and jackets that resemble men's wear. Even the vest is a return to the more masculine look.

The trouser look with the unpressed pleats is usually a much looser pant when it comes to fitting, and they are meant to be worn with shirts that are tucked in, not overblouses. If you wear overblouses with pants, select pants with a smoother look, preferably with darts.

Fitting these pants means being aware of the way they should look. For example, if you simply fit the pants with the darts pressed in place, you will probably be fitting them too tight.

I recommend you baste the darts flat, press them, and keep the bastings in until they are fitted. There must always be more ease for these unpressed pleats or they will pull across the area just below the waistline and balloon out, which is not very flattering.

There are pants for everyone. However, your own figure will determine whether you want them to fit skintight, or whether you will wear them with overblouses to disguise your figure faults.

Woven Fabric Pants

Q. I've been making pants with some degree of perfection. However, I think I'm depending on knitted fabrics. Now I've decided to make some of woven fabrics, and they simply don't fit. I end up with a fold of fabric just below the waistband. What can I do for this?

A. You, like almost everyone who has ever made pants, have forgotten one of the most important measurements. This holds true for skirts as well. You must measure yourself about three inches below the normal waistline. I call this your high hip measurement.

A woman's body is always more curved at this point than the patterns have allowed for, and I've seen many pattern instructions for pants eliminate this measurement altogether. Knits, because of their stretch, will overcome this to some degree, but the real problem comes when working with nonstretch fabrics.

When taking your body measurements, measure the waist, hips, and high hip measurements, as well as the crotch length and total length. You will find that you must make your pattern much straighter from the hips up to the waistline. Now you will have a little excess in the waist, which assures a perfect fit.

Use two rows of machine stitching, a longer stitch than usual, at the waist, one row exactly on the seam allowance and the second row ¼ inch closer to the cut edge. Pull your bobbin threads slightly—this will not give you a gathered look, but will give a little ease instead. Fit the waistband separately; then apply your eased pants to the waistband. You'll be delighted with the results because the pants will now mold to your body and not pull at this crucial area.

Making Pants Narrower

Q. I have been reading that pants will be narrower. Can you tell us how to change our pants that have become outdated?

A. I'll not only answer your questions, but I'll also go into more detail about the narrower pants.

First, as always, I must stress your own figure. Everyone cannot wear extremely tapered pants. You must be fairly slim in the hips for this look. Everyone can wear pants that are straight, but beyond that, you will have to decide individually.

You may turn your pants to the inside and redraw a seamline, beginning at the hips and tapering to the hem. This should be done on the inseam as well as the side seam. Be careful not to curve the seam in too drastically.

Because you are making the lower edges of the pants too narrow to hem properly, you must taper only to the foldline of the hem. Then widen the seam slightly to avoid a puckered hem.

Cuffs on pants are also very popular, and some of you might want to add cuffs to your favorite pattern. You add at least five inches to the length of the pants from the hemline in order to make a two-inch cuff.

Again, cuffs do not look good on wide-legged pants. Cuffs are meant for the more narrow leg. They also are worn slightly shorter than we have been wearing them in the past. The cuffs make the pants more tailored.

For evening, you might want to make narrow satin pants. In any event, for daytime of evening wear, the widths of the narrower pants are from sixteen to twenty inches wide, with an average width of about eighteen inches.

French-Style Slacks

Q. I am looking for a pattern that will enable me to make some French-style slacks. These pants have a waistband, front zipper, cuffed legs and front darts. The front is not tightly fitted, though. In fact, they are loose from waist to hips. What style pattern should I use?

A. I think you are looking for the trouser-type pants that have one or two small pleats in the front which are pressed but not stitched. Usually, you will find a front zipper closing on these patterns, and they will have a waistband because of the pleats. You may have to add cuffs to the pattern, though.

Peg Top Pants

Q. I have read where some pants are referred to as peg top or tapered. What is the difference?

A. Most of these pants either have trouser pleats at the waist or slight gathers. Very few of these pants are fitted tight at the waist and hips by the use of darts. Since these styles vary from extremely narrow at the ankles to just slightly narrower than we have been accustomed to, they will have a tapered effect. The peg top look is achieved by more fullness at the waist, ending in a very narrow cuff, causing it to have a pegged look.

Pants Without Side Seams

Q. Upon close examination, I noticed a pair of ready-made slacks without side seams. I tried them on and loved the way they fit. Why can't we do this with our own sewing? Where can I find a pattern without side seams?

A. Good news for you—you don't have to buy a pattern for this. You can use a favorite pattern you already have.

Simply place the front and back sections of your pants pattern one over the other so the side seams are directly over each other. From the hip area down to the hem, your sides will be perfectly straight.

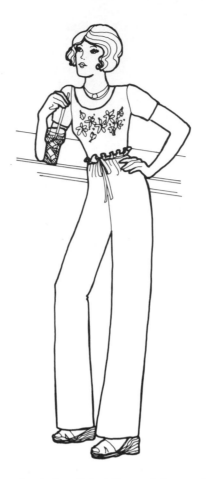

Fig. 12 – Pants without Side Seams

Allow the pattern to spread in order to lay flat at the waist area. You will find the pattern will spread from the waist to the hips with the natural curve intended for the hip area fitting. Make a dart at each side of your pants extending from the waist and gradually tapering to nothing at the hip area. It's as simple as that.

If you are using elastic for the waist or you want to make the drawstring tips, eliminate the darts and the sides will be perfectly straight all the way to the waist. You would have enough ease for the elastic or the drawstring.

Another tip for the drawstring waistline on pants is to allow extra length for the casing at the waist. Some of the pants have a heading (like headings found on curtains). Again, check your measurements to allow enough extra length for this heading and casing. (See figure 12.)

Pocket Problems

Q. Whenever I make pants or a skirt with pockets, I have the same problem. When they are completed and pressed, they look nice and flat. When I wear the garment, the pockets stand away. In other words, they gape open and don't look nice. Any suggestions?

A. Fit your pants with the pocket basted flat. Also, the problem can be solved very easily by adding a little extra width to the pants or skirt. When pockets gape open, it usually means that your garment is too tight at the pocket area.

Creases

Q. When I make slacks, I'm never exactly sure where the crease should be placed. Also, should this crease be machine stitched to keep it sharp?

A. It is actually easier to press the crease in place before the slacks are completed: After you have machine stitched the side seams and the inseams, place the legs of your slacks on the pressing board with the two seams over each other. In front and back, the creases should only come to the crotch area.

As to machine stitching the creases, this isn't usually done on expensive ready-made pants. However, some women do prefer this stitching because it does give the pants the look of being pressed no matter what. You would never see a pair of men's slacks with this crease stitched. I would go by the tailoring you find there.

If in doubt about any details you are going to add to your own clothes, check some better ready-to-wear garments before you forge ahead. It's best to copy their details, since this is what people spend good money for. If you're going to make your clothes, you might as well give them the expensive look rather than trying to make up your own details.

Too Short

Q. I have a problem with ready-made slacks. They are too short in the crotch. What can I do to remedy this situation?

A. If the slacks fit perfectly except for the crotch area, you have a very simple alteration.

Stitch your crotch seam slightly lower, clip the seam allowance and try on. You can always stitch it a second time until it is correct, rather than making the crotch too low, which presents a much more tedious alteration.

Just begin where the slacks curve in at the crotch area. Continue across the inseams of the legs and up to the end of the curve.

Pants Pattern

Q. Try as I may, I have never come up with a perfect fitting pair of pants. I have a pair that I bought that fit me perfectly. Could I rip them apart and cut a pattern from the actual pants?

A. This could be a disaster, or it could be very successful. If you are accurate and careful, it could be done.

I'll give you a few tips. Rip your pants apart carefully. Avoid stretching. Press each piece cautiously. You must maintain the original grain line. Be sure to add a little extra seam allowance since the original seam has frayed from laundering or cleaning.

Be sure the grain line of the original pants is the same as the grain line of your fabric. Also, be sure the fabric is the same as the original. Never use a pair of pants made out of woven fabric as a pattern for some knit fabric. The stretch of the knit would cause completely different results.

Slacks for Dieters

Q. I need to make some slacks. Yet I am on a strict diet and know I will be losing weight. How can I make the slacks fit now without having them bag around the waistline in a few weeks?

A. I would suggest you treat the waistline as if you were applying elastic. Use the more fitted method by stitching your darts in front and back for fitting. Also apply a zipper to the center front or back. I would also suggest you use the one-inch, nonroll elastic in the waistline.

As you lose weight, the area that changes quickest is the waistline. The elastic will keep the pants fitting smoothly. Because you fitted them with darts in the beginning, there won't be too much extra fabric to bulge with gathers as you become smaller.

If you have lost more than two inches in the waistline, you might rip the top of the pants, fit the side seams in closer and continue with the elastic, perhaps tightening it slightly. If you lose many inches, you will find the crotch seam has become too long and loose. This requires opening the inseam, taking in each leg separately, and then restitching the crotch area in one continuous seam. This also shortens the crotch.

A final reward when you have accomplished your goal is to make a new pair of slacks to show off your new body.

Twisted Pant Legs

Q. I use the same pants pattern over and over. Recently I made another pair of knit pants and found that one pant leg twists around almost forty-five degrees. No matter how I press them, the results are the same. What is causing this?

A. I can only tell you about a few tips that usually prevent this twisting. First, you must cut each piece of your knit separately. Next, do not follow the selvage as your grain line. The way to find the grain line is to follow a rib of the knit and baste this from one end to the other.

If you have done these things correctly, it must be the fault of the knitted fabric. Sometimes the heatset process can cause distortions. I'm sure any reputable fabric shop would replace the knit for this reason. They in turn will return it to the manufacturer.

Making Skirts from Pants

Q. I have often seen patterns that include both a long skirt or long pants. I am wondering if it is possible to change a pattern I already have with the long pajama pants into a long skirt?

A. Yes, it is possible and can be done very easily. Since the pajama pants you spoke about would be rather full, and in order to have the same fullness in your skirt, the center front would not be cut on the fold. It would be necessary to have a center front as well as a center back seam.

Place your yardstick on the crotch area of the pants and draw an extended line from the edge of your pattern at the waist to the curve of the crotch, straight down to the hem. This will be done in front as well as back.

Since your cutting line is an extension of the original cutting line, your seamline can be ⅝ inch from the outer edge as usual. Your new skirt should hang beautifully, and is much simpler to achieve than cutting pants from a skirt pattern. I wouldn't advise this since you would only be guessing about the shaping of the crotch area.

Chapter 13
TAILORING

Coats

Q. I would like to make a coat for fall, but don't know how much tailoring experience is necessary. I have made jackets quite successfully. Do you have any tips?

A. Please don't be afraid to make a coat. They are actually much easier to make than suits. First, there is much less fitting with a coat. Second, there is much less detail construction. The only difference is the extra length, which only means sewing a few extra inches.

This is certainly a good time to consider making a coat. It's one part of our wardrobes we all need. The reasons for this are the skirts and dresses that are filling the fashion picture.

We can always wear our short jackets with pants, but for skirts, we need the full-length coats. Be sure to make yours below the knees.

If you haven't done much sewing, choose a solid-colored fabric—preferably wool or a wool blend because they tailor much more nicely. Because of the added bulk of these fabrics, I usually recommend a professional pressing when the garment has been completed, in addition to pressing each step as you do your construction.

If you live in a rather cool climate, you may desire a double-breasted coat. It certainly keeps you warmer because the fronts won't separate.

Because you are working with a larger piece of fabric, keep the design simple—let the real beauty be in the fabric. I'm sure you can make almost any coat for a minimum of $50, and there aren't many ready-mades you can buy for that price.

You can use cashmere or camel's hair and spend more money, but it will still be very minimal compared to the prices of ready-made garments. Begin your sewing well ahead of the change of season so your coat will be ready for cool weather.

Fig. 13 — Coat Lengths

Coat Lengths

Q. I can't believe it, but this is the second time in recent years that I have struggled with a coat, only to find that the next season it was too short. I've never seen a coat yet that had the hem let down that didn't look it. What would you advise as a practical solution?

A. Take heart. Your problem could be worse. In the last few years, the length has changed so that the one or two inches you could let down wouldn't do the trick. Much more length is required. It is almost impossible to lengthen a coat, so, instead, shorten it. (See figure 13.)

Yes, you can make a very fashionable shirt-coat or pant coat as seen in ready-to-wear. These short coats, usually about fingertip length, can be worn beautifully over pants or the new longer skirts. Since all of us are built differently, you may pin the coat up with two different lengths and see which is most flattering. I think you'll end up with a coat that you will love and will wear more than the original.

In the future when making a coat, always make it a few inches longer than the dress length. It is perfectly acceptable and will be wearable if skirts go up or down.

Interfacing for Hems

Q. Is there some kind of interfacing to put in the hem of coats, as well as the hems of the sleeves, to prevent the stitches from showing through?

A. The interfacing you are talking about is called wigan. You can make your own strip of wigan by cutting a bias strip of lightweight, woven interfacing about three inches wide.

After the hem of your coat has been carefully marked (always drop the hem slightly at the center back and gradually curve it up to the side seams), baste the line for the fold of the hem. Hems of coats should be about two inches wide—any wider would create too much bulk.

Place the bias strip of interfacing on the fold or marked line of the hem and catch-stitch it in place at the foldline. The strip will extend from the edge of the facing around to the other front where the facing ends.

Next, fold the hem up, baste near the edge and press the hem lightly. It's advisable to use brown paper under the hem to prevent an indentation.

Cut the strip so that only ½ inch remains above the edge of the hem of the garment. Again, catch-stitch the garment fabric to the top of the strip of interfacing—not catching in the coat itself, just the hem. Next, catch-stitch the interfacing only (that extends above the hem) to the seams of your coat. The lining will hold the rest in place.

Proceed the same way with the sleeves of any suit or coat that will have a finished lining. You'll love the extra body and the professional look it gives your garment by eliminating those unsightly stitches from showing through. Of course, this is only practical in a lined garment.

Sport Coats

Q. I have made several sport coats for my husband with reasonably good luck. The lapels seem to be in the right place and roll back nicely until the jacket is buttoned—then the fronts gape and stand away from the body. Before I try another one, can you tell me what I am doing wrong?

A. I will let you in on a little tip that I learned from a wonderful tailor many years ago, and it really works.

Place a strip of twill tape on the roll-line of the lapels, holding it slightly tighter than the garment. This little ease will not cause wrinkles, but it will keep the jacket closer to the body to avoid gaping and will also tend to make the lapel roll nicer.

The tape should extend from the front edge of the garment to just past the place where the collar joins the garment. Hand whip each side of the tape with tiny stitches to the interfacing of the jacket.

Jacket Lining

Q. When I line a jacket, should I put it entirely together and then attach it to the garment, or should I do the sleeves separately? If so, do I use my gathering stitches in the cap of the sleeves to get rid of the excess ease before I put it in the garment?

A. There is probably a difference between some pattern instructions and some teachers on this subject. Personally, I prefer leaving the shoulder seams open on the lining and not applying the sleeve linings to the lining itself.

I stitch the lining to the edges of the facing, and then baste the front edge of the shoulder lining to the shoulder seams of my jacket. Next, I bring the back lining over the shoulder and slip stitch invisibly all across the back facing as well.

Then I baste the armhole of the linings permanently to the armholes of my garment.

Prepare the sleeves as follows. Simply machine stitch the cap of the sleeve with your regular stitch on the seamline. It is not necessary to pull the ease up as you do with your sleeves. The machine stitching on a single layer of fabric actually eases the fabric enough. Turn the seam allowance over on the sleeve lining and pin in place, easing wherever necessary; then complete by slip stitching invisibly.

When it comes to finishing the hem of the lining, be sure to add a little ease so the sleeve doesn't pull when you move. Always remember that the lining of a garment must be slightly looser than the garment itself or it will pull and look unattractive from the outside of the garment.

Chapter 14
PRESSING

Achieve Sharp Pressing

Q. I find that when sewing with the new fabrics, it is impossible to achieve sharp pressing. No matter what I do, the fabric seems to pucker slightly. When I do use the press cloth and extra pressure in pressing, there are always marks where the seam allowances show from the right side of the garment. I am very confused about pressing procedures on synthetic fabrics. What do you recommend?

A. As soon as a seam has been stitched, press it in the stitched position before opening the seams. Then lightly press the seams open before doing any heavy pressing. If you are going to press the seams or any area that needs a sharper press, use a dampened press cloth and a hot iron. Always experiment with your fabric first. Each one requires a different heat.

I usually keep strips of brown paper (regular grocery sacks are perfect) near my pressing area. Slip a strip of paper under each side of the seam allowances before doing your hard pressing. You will be delighted with the results. It completely eliminates the marks formerly left by the seam allowance.

As soon as the hem has been marked accurately, baste evenly, slip the paper under the cut edge of the hem and press thoroughly before hand stitching the hem. You will eliminate the stitches that would show if you pressed after hemming.

Jacket Pressing

Q. It seems like every time I make an unlined, loose-fitting jacket, it falls open all the way down the facing instead of only at the lapel area. Is there any solution to this, other than a heavy pressing at the lapel line?

A. When you sew the edge of the facing to the garment, don't hold it flat—roll the lapel over your hand the way you want it to lay and pin it in position. Tack the facing lightly, as the buttons and buttonholes will hold the balance of the facing in the correct position.

To shape the lapel area, steam press the lapel and collar area from the inside. When it is fairly moist, turn the garment over and finger shape the area.

Hold the fabric in position until it is dry, and your lapels should roll beautifully and stay in place.

Pants Crease

Q. Whenever I press the crease in the pants I have made, the crease seems to come to the end of the front darts which makes a pucker at the end of the dart. What am I doing wrong?

A. You are pressing the crease up too far. The crease should never interfere with the darts. The darts at the front of your pants should be very short and small, not longer than about three to four inches. Taper them so fine that there is no pucker at the end.

When pressing the crease in the pants legs, end the crease about seven inches below the waistline, front and back.

Press Seams on Wrong Side

Q. When constructing a knit garment, I am in doubt about the pressing of seams. When I press on the right side of the knit, I am getting a shiny, ironed-on look and the impression of the seams shows. Pattern instructions don't tell us how to press. Do you have some suggestions?

A. Never press on the right side of ANY fabric. Always press on the wrong side, lightly at first, most often with a steam iron. If more pressing is necessary, you may use a dampened press cloth and use a slightly warmer iron.

Unless you are a real pro with your sewing, it is usually advisable to take your finished garment to a professional for the final pressing. This can often make the difference between a garment that has that "loving hands at home" look and one that is purchased. Pressing is one of the most important details of any garment.

Synthetics Require Cooler Iron

Q. I was pressing my new evening gown after I had completed it and the iron stuck to the fabric and caused it to pucker in one spot. How can I be sure what setting to use on the iron to avoid this?

A. I'm very sorry this had to happen to you, but it does give me a chance to caution all of you about pressing synthetic fabrics. I imagine your gown was made of Qiana®, which is a trademark by DuPont for nylon. Nylon, like other synthetics, requires a much cooler iron for pressing than the true fibers such as cotton, linen or wool.

My best advice is to always pretest your pressing on a scrap of your fabric before you forge ahead. Another word of warning is never to press on the right side of any fabric.

You might be able to lightly press over the puckered part of your gown on the wrong side with a cooler iron. However, such a mark usually destroys the fibers, causing them to shrink up, and there is rarely anything you can do.

Chapter 15
FASHION DETAILS

Lettuce Leaf Edging

Q. I see lettuce leaf edging everywhere on those slinky knits and want to do the same for my own dresses and blouses. Would you give these instructions?

A. First, the fabric must be cut on the bias if it is a woven fabric. If it is a knit, it doesn't need to be cut on the bias because of the give of the knit.

The lettuce leaf hem is done on the edge of the garment. You will not need facings or hem allowances.

Most of you will be able to follow these instructions as long as your sewing machine has a zigzag stitch. Fold over ½ inch of the raw or cut edge and press slightly. Use the narrowest width zigzag stitch and keep your stitch fairly small so the stitching will look like an overcast edge rather than a zigzag stitch.

As you stitch the very edge of the fold, pull your fabric. The more you pull, the more curly the edge will appear. After your stitching is completed, carefully cut away the excess half-inch you turned back. Cut very close to the stitching and you should be very pleased with your lettuce leaf hem.

Bias scarfs can also be stitched the same way. They make beautiful fill-ins for shirts and shirt dresses and also make excellent gifts.

Lettuce Leaf Edging in Knit Fabrics

Q. I tried making the lettuce leaf edging, and it doesn't look like it should. Where did I go wrong? I took it for granted that the fabric must be cut on the bias and then applied as a ruffle to my garment. Is this right?

A. There are different ways of making the lettuce leaf edging that has become so popular. It was started by young designers who used this finish for hems and necklines of knits.

When you are working with knits, they do not have to be cut on the bias. There is a natural stretch quality in knits. As you are stitching the edges, you must use a wider bite or stitch width for your zigzag stitches because they must cover the edge of the fabric.

As you stitch the edge, be sure to pull the fabric tight in the area you are working with, a little at a time.

If you are trying to get this finish with woven fabrics, it's a different technique. First, with woven fabrics, the area you are working with for the lettuce leaf edging must be cut on the bias. Otherwise, there is no way you can stretch a woven piece of fabric enough for the curled edge.

When working with very sheer fabrics such as organza and chiffons, turn the edge under and press (again these edges must be cut on the bias). Next, zigzag the edges right on the fold, stretching the fabric as you stitch.

After the edges have been stitched, cut away the excess fabric you originally turned under. Cut very close to the stitching so it will look like it was done on a single layer of fabric.

Perfect Pockets

To make perfect pockets, prepare the pockets perfectly before applying them to the garment. Stitch and turn the hem area. If pocket is to be topstitched, you must stitch the top of the pocket at this time.

Next, machine stitch around the outer edges of the pocket (single layer) exactly on the seamline. If the fabric is too lightweight, you might consider backing it with a lightweight press-on interfacing, which would have to be done before any other steps are taken. The machine stitching you have done will be a guide for the exact outer edges of your pocket.

Notch out the excess fabric from the curved lower corners and trim the seam allowance slightly. Next, baste the seam allowance back to the pocket, turning the pocket on your stitching line. Carefully press the seam allowance flat. Your pockets should be exactly the same size and look perfect.

Cut small pieces of Stitch Witchery and place them on a line just inside the placement marks for your pocket on your garment. Carefully place your pocket on top of the Stitch Witchery, according to your marks. Lightly press pocket in place.

You are now ready to machine stitch the pocket to the garment. I think you will find with this method that the pocket will not shift out of position, but will hold in place while you do your stitching. Sometimes a little extra step can prevent hours of ripping and doing over.

Rounded Corners

Q. My difficulty is getting nice rounded corners on pockets and curves at the hem of skirts. Somehow, mine always have little angles instead of a nice smooth curve. What should I do?

A. One of the easiest ways to keep these edges rounded is to machine stitch on the cut edge of the curves with a wide zigzag stitch, stitching over a separate double thread. After the curve has been stitched, pull the separated thread lightly. Don't pull too tight, just enough so that the cut edge will fit smoothly when turned up on the ⅝ inch seamline. This is easy to do, and you'll be delighted with the professional results. Press these edges until smooth before applying to the garment.

On heavier fabrics such as denim or firm cottons, you may want to trim the seam allowance to ¼ inch at the curves. Continue as above, zigzag stitching on the cut edge. Pull up the extra thread until the curve is smooth. By trimming the excess fabric away, this edge will lose most of its bulk and will press flat for application. Knowing when to clip and trim can save many hours of frustration. These are little details that pattern instructions often fail to mention.

Reversible Skirts

Q. I would like to make some reversible summer skirts like the kind you see in catalogues or boutique shops. Can any two fabrics be combined, and what type of binding works best to cover the outer edges?

A. Yes, just about any two fabrics can be used for your reversible skirt, provided they aren't too heavy and stiff. Make each one separately; then baste them together at the outer edges, wrong sides together. This will enclose the seams and darts.

You could use a foldover braid to contrast the prints in cotton or polyester. If you use the braid, be sure to preshrink it and don't pull it as you apply it to the outer edges.

You can also cut bias strips of one of your fabrics. Cut your strips at least two inches wide. Apply to one side by machine, fold over, and hand whip the other side so that they will both look perfect.

These skirts are usually finished with the same braid at the top, eliminating a waistband and allowing extra length to tie at the waist.

You surely can save lots of money on these skirts because they require so little fabric. They are usually $30 to $40 ready-made.

Border Print

Q. I found a beautiful border print that I would like to use for a skirt. However, if I cut it up with side seams, it will spoil the lovely large paisley pattern at the hem. Is there any way this skirt can be cut without side seams and also without all the extra bulk from this additional width of fabric at the waist?

A. Check the width of your pattern at the hemline. If there are six seam allowances, you must also add that. You will know just how much fabric to purchase. You really won't need a pattern to make this skirt.

Eliminate any side seam. Simply plan your cutting so that the center back seam will come out beautifully with the print. Apply your zipper to the center back seam.

Next, fold the fabric so that you can see where the sides will be. You will make fairly deep darts at each side from the waist, tapering to nothing about seven inches below the waist. This will form the natural curve that would have been in the pattern if you had cut the side seams.

To eliminate excess fullness, mark and stitch two extra darts at each side of the center front and center back. These darts will not be as deep as the side seams, but taper them nicely to avoid a bulge at the ends.

After you have taken out all this excess fabric in darts, your next step will be to stitch your two rows of machine basting in order to ease up the gathers onto your waistband. Check your figure and be sure you are placing the ease in the most flattering places.

I think you will love this dirndl skirt. It won't be too full at the waist, and will still give you a very new look without destroying the design. I definitely recommend a waistband with the dirndl skirt I have described, instead of an elastic casing. With the elastic casing, there would be too much bulk due to the darts.

Make Something Beautiful with Border Fabrics

Q. I have such a desire to use some of the beautiful fabrics with a border at one edge, yet there are so few patterns where a border is used that I always get cold feet. Why is it that we see these things in ready-made garments and yet are afraid to try them on our own?

A. It takes a little imagination to use unusual fabrics. This is the real joy of sewing. You can let yourself go and see what you can create with unusual fabrics.

Border fabric may be used as a shirt jacket with the border at the lower edge of the jacket and the sleeves. It can be used at the hemline of pants or skirts, provided that the skirts are simple A-line (almost straight at the side seams).

Bordered fabrics are lovely in many dress patterns. Just keep in mind that the hem must be almost straight for the borders. I have also seen the border beginning at the waistline instead of the hem. The same holds true for dresses and jackets—the right kind of border can begin at the shoulder instead of the hem. If your fabric has a banding effect, this could be applied for center front bands, cuffs, and collars.

These are just some suggestions for you to think about, but by all means, don't avoid these lovely fabrics—just allow enough time to plan before cutting.

Fig. 14 — Border Fabrics

Border Fabrics

Q. On a recent trip, my husband bought me a beautiful piece of fabric with a border print. My favorite pattern has side front and side back seams with a flared hem. Will this pattern work for my bordered material? How can I keep the hem even?

A. Bordered fabrics are so beautiful. You must engineer your pattern carefully before cutting. Ordinarily, a flared skirt or one with many seams is not suitable for borders because the pattern is broken too often. The flared skirt would prevent the pattern from having an even design at the hemline.

If you want to use this flared skirt pattern, you might change the border and use it at the top of the dress as a yoke design, for the sleeves, collars or scarf. I have seen borders down the front of a dress and at the side on a double-breasted design.

Plan carefully to get the most eye-catching design possible. It might help to sketch your pattern with the design in different areas. You might be limited by the direction of the border design. This is much too broad an area to come up with a single answer. Just play around and have fun. Borders can be a real challenge. (See figure 14.)

Seam Pipings

Q. I've noticed many pipings inserted in seams this year to add or pick up a contrasting color. Whenever I do this, the piping is never even. What advice can you give me?

A. The instructions would depend on whether you are using a corded piping or bias tape as a cording. We will begin with the bias tape idea first. Press the folded edges of the bias tape open. Fold the bias tape in half lengthwise, matching the raw edges exactly, and press flat.

Place the folded bias tape on the right side of the garment section and match the raw edges of the tape to the raw edges of your garment. Machine baste in place exactly on the seamline. Before proceeding, check to see that exactly the same width of piping is showing everywhere.

Next, pin both sections of the garment together with the piping in between and stitch your seam. Do this machine stitching directly over the basting stitches which will serve as a guide. Press all the seams to one side.

If you are using a cording in your piping, cut the fabric on the bias and place the cord on the fabric (using string or heavy cording, depending on the width you desire). Fold bias over the cord and machine stitch very close to the cording. Use the zipper foot for this to get close enough.

You should have ⅝ inch excess bias from the stitching line to the cut edges. Cut and remove any excess. Next, place the corded piping on the right side of your fabric, cut edges together, and machine baste as above. Check to be sure your cording is perfectly even. Then place the facing or other piece of garment over this, encasing the piping between the two. Machine stitch permanently from the basting side of the garment using these machine basting stitches as a guide to a perfect seam. Always ease in tight at inner curves.

Tunics from Short Dresses

Q. Since the dresses are longer this year, why can't we make tunics out of our dresses that are too short and make contrasting pants for them?

A. This is an excellent idea if the fabric is suitable. Actually, you could make an evening tunic out of your dressier fabrics. Since most tunic tops are slit at the sides, you can open the side seams as far as you desire. Then add a long skirt or pants to coordinate your tops. This is one way we can recycle our clothes and get some additional wear from them. (See figure 15.)

Fig. 15 – Tunics from Short Dresses

Machine-Stitched Hem

Q. I recently finished a circular skirt and tried to machine stitch the hem in two rows as you suggested. Now the edge curls up in spots. The stitching isn't nice and smooth but looks puckered between the rows. What did I do wrong?

A. Any circular or bias edge to be topstitched must be handled even more carefully than straight edges to prevent its pulling out of shape.

It would probably help if you basted the hem first to be sure it is even, and press slightly. Next, stitch the outside stitching first, that is, the row of stitching closest to the fold of the hem. Be sure not to pull as you stitch. Instead, hold your fingers on each side of the presser foot to prevent stretching.

For the second row of stitching, which is about ¼ inch from the first row, you must carefully watch your stitching line. If you see the fabric pushing ahead of the presser foot and causing puckers between the rows of stitching, stop, rip back and begin again. You must hold the fabric very firm. Also, stitch rather slowly.

Straight edges to be machine stitched are much easier to keep even. There is still a chance that you could stretch the edges. Always use your regular thread and about ten to twelve stitches per inch, not long stitches. Unless your stitching is perfect, avoid contrasting colored thread.

Machine-stitched edges are very much in fashion today and compensate for the lack of construction that would ordinarily keep a garment in shape. Watch what the designers do to perfect this detail.

Corduroy on the Bias

Q. I just saw a corduroy skirt cut on the bias. I was always taught that the nap should go in one direction. What is correct?

A. Rules are meant to be broken. When it comes to designers, they will never stop being different. The most popular corduroy today is the wider wale.

Yes, I have seen these bias skirts of corduroy, and I find them very attractive. I have also seen them cut on the cross-grain for jackets and skirts. Why not have a little fun with this very rugged, sturdy, classic fabric and turn it into a conversation piece.

You will still watch the grain. In other words, all the pieces of your pattern will still be cut in the same direction, whether it is bias, cross-grain or whatever. If you are cutting it with the normal grainline, I like to cut it against the nap so that the color is deeper and it doesn't flatten out when you sit on it.

There is another popular corduroy which is a no-wale cord that looks and feels like velveteen.

Button Last Button on Placket

Q. When there is a placket closing with buttons that extends down the center front of a dress, ending just below the waistline, I have difficulty trying to prevent the placket from pulling out due to strain when the garment is put on and taken off. Do you have a tip on how to handle this?

A. The little tip that works beautifully is to keep the last button buttoned at all times. It might be necessary when sewing it on to catch a few threads of the buttonhole as well so that you really can't unbutton it.

If the placket is done perfectly, it is barely held together. Therefore, we must do everything to avoid any extra strain. The last button is usually only for fashion or balance. It is not necessary to open it for comfort.

Bias Stretches

Q. Does the bias-cut skirt or dress stretch or grow in woven fabrics? You have mentioned that it does with knits.

A. Yes, any part of a garment cut on the bias in woven fabric will certainly stretch somewhat. It is always advisable to allow any bias area to relax and stretch out to its fullest before completing the garment.

As to knit garments, some of them will continue to grow and get longer. If you find this happening, it's best to fold the garment and allow it to remain flat in a drawer instead of on a hanger. With many new fabrics, there are no set rules to go by. Each garment and each fabric can present a new set of problems and must be treated individually.

Covering Buttonhole Mistakes

Q. I am heartbroken. After buying some beautiful fabric and having it made up, I found that the machine buttonholes on the jacket were so slanted that they looked crooked. Is there anything I can do to correct this?

A. This was indeed an unfortunate experience for you. Sew an extra strip of fabric over the front for a band detail, perhaps on the bias, and do not add new buttonholes. It will look like a fly-front closing and the buttonholes would be covered under the fly. Of course, you would have to use very flat buttons.

Another suggestion would be to cover the buttonholes with frogs or the new toggle closings, depending on how sporty the garment is. You could even put a strip of leather or Ultrasuede® down the front with machine-stitched detail to hide the error. Use your creative ideas—perhaps they will enhance the garment.

A good rule to remember in the future is: When there is a whole line of buttonholes, DON'T cut any of them open until you have checked the positioning on all of them and made sure they are all the same size. They can be ripped out and restitched if an error is caught before cutting—it is impossible after they have been cut.

Vertical Buttonholes

Q. Why do the patterns have buttonholes placed vertically instead of the conventional horizontal placement?

A. There is a very good reason why the buttonholes are worked vertically on the tailored shirts and shirt dresses. The answer concerns the front band you will almost always find on this type of classic, tailored garment. When there is a narrow band on the front, it is impossible to do anything except place the buttonholes at the center of the band in a vertical position.

Try making the buttonholes closer to the size of the buttons. They might be a little more difficult to button, but they will not pop open.

If you carefully look through your pattern books, you will find a few tailored garments without the front band. These buttonholes may be worked horizontally.

If you have trouble with the garments you purchase, you may hand sew each buttonhole together for a closer fit to the size of the button. Do this from the wrong side.

Cowl Neckline

Q. I just completed a long dress with a cowl or draped neckline. The picture on the pattern looked so graceful and soft; however, the neckline on my dress is stiff and doesn't fall into folds. Should this have been cut on the bias?

A. The cowl neckline, which is really a draped neckline and so very popular today, must be made of soft drapable fabric or you will loose the effect. I imagine the fabric you used was stiff instead of soft and flexible. Any fabric will drape more easily if it is cut on the bias. However, some patterns don't require this.

It's a good idea to check the kinds of fabrics recommended on the back of the pattern envelope to be sure you have selected a suitable fabric.

Keeping Belts Smooth

Q. So many of the styles today call for a long, tie belt to be made out of the same fabric as the dress. I have tried this many, many times and always have the same disastrous results. The tie turns into a skinny rolled-over belt that is unattractive. Is there some way to keep these belts from turning over?

A. I couldn't agree more. I have not only had this happen to me personally, but have seen this on any number of women. It is caused by a number of factors, mainly the way we are built. Unless you are thin and straight through the waistline area, the tie belt is certainly going to fold over and look unattractive.

Measure your waistline, deduct about two or three inches and cut a strip of web-type belting. It isn't too heavy and is guaranteed to be nonroll. This can be attached to the belt facing at each end. Be sure to center it on the belt.

Next, fold the belt with right sides together and complete your stitching. When the belt is turned to the right side, the belting won't show. When you place it around your waist, it will stay nice and straight because of the belting. However, it will be soft enough to tie in a nice bow at the waist because you didn't apply the belting to the entire belt.

Try it—it has certainly answered my needs. Hope it helps you, too.

Tissue Paper Keeps Fabric from Stretching

Q. I am making a full-length lightweight knit dress with intricate embroidery around the hemline. What is the best way to keep the fabric taut while doing the embroidery around the hemline without stretching the fabric out of shape?

A. You will probably have to use embroidery hoops for your work. I would suggest you use a sheet of tissue paper under the area you are working on when you apply the embroidery hoops. The tissue will keep the fabric from stretching. It is simple to pull away from the back of the fabric when you have completed your handwork.

Keep shifting the hoops as you go around the entire hem, putting new tissue under each area. This will work when doing machine embroidery on T-shirts or any other type of knits that would ordinarily stretch out of shape.

Bias-Striped Fabrics

Q. Why do so many patterns tell you they are not suitable for bias-striped fabrics? Apparently you could not use a regular collar, but couldn't this be cut on the bias and have pleasing results?

A. Fabrics printed with bias stripes and design take a little more thought than the average sewer is willing to give. This fabric is usually found only in ready-to-wear.

There is no valid reason why most patterns cannot be cut with this fabric, but you should avoid raglan sleeves or a shawl collar that is cut in one with the facing. A regular shirt collar can be cut on the bias, and this would give a horizontal stripe effect which should work well.

The press-on interfacing used on the wrong side of the top collar would stabilize the fabric and avoid stretching. Choose patterns with very little detail and few pattern sections. This will allow the beauty of the bias stripes to show to the best advantage. Of course, a bias-cut garment would not work either.

A tip I have used often that works with many unusual fabrics is as follows:

On every pattern work sheet is a miniature sketch of each piece of your pattern. On a plain piece of paper, draw either diagonal stripes or borders or whatever, and place these miniature pieces of your pattern on the paper. You will be able to see exactly how each piece of your pattern will look on your fabric. You can actually trace the lines and pin the small pieces together.

At this point, you can make decisions about the choice of pattern without touching your fabric. If you don't like the effect, simply choose another pattern.

Make a Dickey

Q. Do you have a pattern for a dickey—the kind that you can make from a shirt fabric and not knit?

A. There is no need for a special pattern. You can create your own dickey from any regular pattern. I have checked out the ready-made ones, and they are usually only about chest length, front and back, with a variety of necklines.

Just use your regular dress or blouse pattern and cut the neckline exactly the same, cut shoulders to almost the armhole, and cut the length about twelve inches from the shoulder. Finish the outer edges (which you have rounded) with a narrow hem, or pink for a smoother effect.

I personally prefer a dickey to come to the waistline. If you would like this kind, measure from shoulder to waist for the correct length. You might make the dickey slightly wider to include any darts for bustline shaping.

Measure your waistline with a narrow strip of grosgrain ribbon. Center the front and back to the ribbon. The sides will be just the ribbon. Hook the ribbon together at the center front.

You will find that by making the dickey longer, it will stay firmly in place and not ride up like the shorter ones will.

Dickeys are great for filling in a neckline that is suddenly too bare, or for dressing up or down any garment. Your choice of fabrics can range from sweater knits to satin or chiffon.

Smock Jacket Trim Suggestions

Q. I have seen ready-made smock-type jackets and I want to make some for myself. These jackets usually don't open all the way to the waist—they are the slip-over type and only close with a lacing. How can I find the right kind of trim to use for lacings, and how can I get the machine-made round eyelets for the lacings?

A. There are a few details used in ready-to-wear that are difficult to copy exactly. If you can't copy them to the last inch, you must substitute other trims or details and be happy with the effect, which will be almost the same.

If you can't find the cording, make your own out of your fabric. I have seen this self-trim used for lacings in better ready-to-wear.

As for round eyelets that are often found in ready-to-wear, if you live in or near a large city, you will usually find a company that makes covered buttons and belts. They have the machinery needed to make the round eyelets for you. If it isn't possible to find this in your city, you will have to substitute by making small buttonholes. It will work just as well, since the overall effect is what you are looking for.

Keep Waistline from Bunching

Q. The sheath dresses without a waistline always seem to bunch at the waist for me. They look fine when I've just placed the belt in position, but the minute I move, my dress bunches up and looks terrible. Is there any way to keep the waistline at the waist?

A. Yes, there is a rather simple way to keep the waistline in place. Try your dress on; then tie a string very tightly around the waistline at the exact place you would wear a belt. Mark this line with pins in several spots as a guide. When you take off your dress, baste around the entire waistline according to where you placed your pins.

Turn your dress to the wrong side, use a zigzag stitch and stitch over a long piece of thin, round elastic where you basted. Leave the ends long, try the dress on again, even out the fullness, and make it as tight as you desire. I wouldn't recommend it be too tight, just an easy fit. Secure the ends of the elastic and from this point on, you won't have any worries.

You'll find the dress will stay in place beautifully, and the ease of the gathers will be exactly where you want them.

Applying Binding

Q. I saw a lovely black suit that was bound around the edges with black satin. I have done quite a lot of sewing, and I'm not afraid to tackle this detail. I'm not sure if I should finish all the outer edges by turning the facings, or if I should place the satin on the cut edges. If I should do the latter, could you give me a few tips?

A. I usually prefer binding over the cut edges of a garment to eliminate some of the bulk. However, this will depend on your fabrics. The binding you use must not be too thin or lightweight. If it is, you will see any irregularities in the edge of the garment, and the binding won't look nice and padded.

Whatever you use for a binding, be sure it is heavier than the fabric for the garment. The strips for binding must be cut on the bias to give a nice, tight edge.

Just a review of instructions for binding: If you are going to bind the cut edges, you must place your facings with the wrong side touching the interfacing. In other words, your facing will be right side out, as will the garment fabric.

Pin all these cut edges together carefully and machine stitch through all layers about ¾ inch from the edges. Carefully cut the original ⅝-inch seam allowance off. You won't need it since you aren't turning your facings in the ordinary way.

When applying satin binding, place right sides together and machine stitch this seam only. Your machine stitching will be determined by the width of the binding you desire. When turning over the other edge of the binding, you will slip stitch this edge in place. The binding must come to the cut edge of the garment to look professional. Never allow the binding to go past the edge of the garment.

These details are lovely, but they do take a little extra time, so be sure to practice on some sample fabric before you begin.

Small Details Make Clothes Unique

Q. On a recent shopping trip, I was examining some expensive clothes and noticed that both skirts and pants had two short zippers, approximately four inches long, on each side seam instead of using a seven-inch zipper in either the front or the back. What is the reasoning behind this, and what are we going to do when we try to copy this style and can't find these zippers?

A. This is just one of the little details that make designer clothes unique. Possibly the real reason is so that the zipper will not show below short jackets.

At any rate, this is not too difficult to achieve yourself. Use your seven-inch zippers and apply them to a four-inch opening.

After the applications, fasten the end of the four-inch length securely by overcasting it several times across the zipper track so the key of the zipper can't possibly go beyond this. Clip off the end of the zipper, leaving about one extra inch of length for security.

Underlining Chiffon

Q. I want to make one of the sheer printed chiffon blouses, but I don't care for the complete see-through. Is there any way I can make this blouse a little more opaque without losing the effect of the chiffon?

A. I suggest underlining the bodice front and back only with a layer of solid-colored polyester chiffon. This is actually more like a georgette and much easier to handle than the old silk chiffon of years ago.

Place several colors under your print to see which one is the most effective. If you wish the color to remain closest to your original color and not look entirely different from the unlined areas, try using a beige (skin tone) chiffon.

You'll even find it easier to work with and I know you'll be pleased with the results. You will not change the beautiful soft look of the chiffon.

Practice Topstitching

Q. I have tried using topstitching on sportswear. My problem is not the machine stitching. Fortunately, it turns out perfect. My problem is that between the outside edges and the stitching which I have about ⅜ inch from the edge, there are diagonal folds of fabric. It looks as if the top layer of fabric was stretched. Can you give me some tips on topstitching?

A. You have diagnosed your own problem. Yes, you have stretched the top layer of fabric. The natural action of the presser foot of your machine has a tendency to push the top layer of fabric ahead of the second layer.

You can correct this by carefully placing your forefingers on each side of the presser foot and gently pushing or feeding the fabric into the machine without allowing it to move out of position.

The minute you begin to see these wrinkles forming, stop, rip the last few stitches and begin again. I would suggest that everyone practice topstitching through the normal two layers of fabric as often as necessary until you have perfected the technique.

Topstitching is very important on today's fabrics and fashions. It will keep polyester fabrics nice and sharp at the edges. Most topstitching is done with your regular machine stitching thread. Often two rows are used; the first row at the exact edge of the garment, the second stitching about ¼ inch in from the first row.

Buttonhole twist is a heavier thread and more difficult to use on most sewing machines. This is beautiful for the heavier-type fabrics, but only if you have mastered the ability to stitch perfectly. For buttonhole twist, I recommend a size 16 or 18 needle to accommodate the size of the thread.

Ribbon Trim for Sweater

Q. I would love to use a beautiful woven, jaccard-type ribbon trim on a sweater. The ones I have seen are very costly, and even though the trim I plan to use is expensive, I can still save almost half the price of the ready-made ones. How can I get this straight, flat ribbon to look right as it curves around the neckline?

A. I would like to give you a few extra tips in addition to those for curved areas. First, be sure to ease the ribbon to the sweater. Remember, the sweater has built-in stretch factors the trim doesn't have, so it is quite easy to pull the trim too tight, causing it to pucker. I imagine you are planning to put the trim straight up the front edges and continue around the neckline.

After you have completed one side of the front, you must make a perfect miter at the corner. Next, carefully pin the outside edge (the one farthest from the neckline) smoothly to the sweater around the curve. You will be able to see just how often you must make small darts in your ribbon—usually about ¼ inch deep at the neckline tapering to nothing at the edges of the ribbon.

Pin these darts in again, being careful not to pull too tight. Unpin the trim from the sweater, mark darts on the wrong side of ribbon, machine stitch, and press. If you have stitched these carefully, you will have a nice curve for the neckline.

Again pin loosely in place, miter at the other corner and continue trim to hem of sweater. To attach trim, take small, invisible hand stitches. Do not pull tight; keep thread rather loose.

This same technique will work anytime you are applying trim that is not stretchable to a curved edge.

Chapter 16
SEWING FOR WEDDINGS

Be an Individual

Q. What makes the mother of the bride often the worst-dressed person in the wedding party?

A. This is a tough question to answer, but an important one to remember if you will be faced with this in the future. First, mothers often try too hard to coordinate with the pastels chosen for the bridesmaids. Consider yourselves as individuals who should not clash with the rest of the party. Often pastels are not flattering to more mature figures.

Speaking of figures, check that out first to see what you have to work with. If you are lumpy or thick through the middle, you certainly won't want one of the lightweight knits that tend to cling.

Even though most of us have discarded wearing foundation garments due to the construction of today's clothes, perhaps you should consider one for this important occasion when you will be seen from the front as well as the back. Those little rounded areas aren't too attractive in certain fabrics. You also should consider the color. The lighter the color, the larger you will look. You can keep the color theme by selecting darker shades of any color.

Chiffon is used so often as a toga-type coverlet, I would suggest you make this float as long as possible for a more slender look. The prints of the chiffons also tend to disguise figure faults. Many designer gowns come with matching unconstructed full-length simple coats in the same fabric. This is a beautiful disguise that adds length and diminishes width.

If you have chosen a knit, look at yourself carefully and be sure it doesn't cling in the wrong places. Perhaps a full-length slip of lightweight taffeta will keep the fabric from clinging to your figure.

I think most women forget there is a generation gap. You want to look as attractive as you can for your age and not try to look as young as the bridal party.

Keep your gown as simple as possible, with flattering lines for your particular figure. Choose a color that will enhance your skin, hair, and body, and you will surely come out as a winner.

I would rather see a lovely, shirtwaist gown on a larger woman than one that exposes heavy arms, bust, or whatever. The matter of bridal dressing is a very individual thing and must be treated as such for your own self-confidence.

Dressing the Mother of the Bride

Q. My daughter is having a large wedding, and my question concerns my gown for the wedding. I would like to wear a long sleeveless gown with a matching capelet to cover the arms. I am concerned about the finished edges of the capelet. Should I finish it in a lettuce leaf-type hem or with ostrich feathers?

A. When it comes to weddings, I do have a very definite stand. Everyone is trying to steal the show from the bride, which is unfair.

My opinion would be to wear a lovely, becoming color in a subdued fashion. In other words, keep it simple. If the fabric is a knit, you may finish the edges of the capelet in the popular lettuce leaf edging. I feel ostrich feathers would be much too theatrical for an afternoon wedding.

One of the most beautiful weddings I have ever attended was done entirely in white—yes, the mothers of the bride and groom, the bridesmaids, and flower girl. In this way, no one took any spotlight away from the bride. I'm not advocating everyone have a white wedding, but I am suggesting that everyone in the wedding dress as a background for the bride instead of trying to be the center of attention.

Start with Classic Design

Q. Do you have any information on patterns for wedding gowns and bridesmaids' dresses? We are planning a wedding for my daughter and the pattern books do not have enough variety.

A. Since most bridal and bridesmaids' gowns are classic designs, I would use the patterns for your guide. Then, purchase the current brides' magazines (there are several on the market), and use these as your guide for variation in laces, fabrics, and trims.

I have looked through both and feel that almost any gown you see in the brides' magazines can be duplicated from a combination of patterns.

The dimension of the fabric makes such a difference in your gowns. I actually prefer a simple pattern without too much detail. The beauty is in the fabric and trim as well as color combinations. Keep the lines simple, don't overdo the details, and you'll have beautiful, professional results.

Don't finish the hems of the dresses until the last minute. Also, most brides lose weight at the last minute, so be prepared to make last minute changes at the waistline area.

Tablecloth Lace

Q. My daughter has seen the fabric she'd like to use for her wedding gown. It's called tablecloth lace. It's washable and made of polyester. Do you think this will work, and how should a lining be applied? Also, would she use a lace veil?

A. I'm sure the washable lace you are referring to will work beautifully for the wedding gown. Usually, a complete lace gown doesn't need any enhancement on the veil. I would suggest you keep it as simple as possible so as not to distract from the gown.

Many lace gowns have only the bodice underlined. This means the bodice and the lining would be basted together and constructed as one piece of fabric. However, the skirt is usually more beautiful if you make the lace and lining separate.

When finishing seams of lace fabric, there are several ways of construction. I usually suggest stitching a second row of machine stitching about ¼ inch from the seamline (do not open the seams); then you can cut the raw edges fairly close to the second stitching. The seam will appear very narrow and will not be noticeable. You may use French seams if you prefer.

When making the lining for the skirt, attach it to the bodice seam at the waist or at the empire line and let it hang free from the skirt. If you wish both the lining and the lace to stand out a little, apply narrow hair braid to the hem of each. Wedding gowns take more time to make than most people realize. It is wise to begin early.

Fuller Skirts

Q. I'm making the bridesmaids' dresses for my daughter's wedding. She has chosen a pattern that calls for a full, flared skirt that is made of sheer fabric and worn with a full slip. The gore patterns we have seen are not full enough. I'm afraid they will not stand away from the slip as I would like. Do you have any suggestions?

A. The best thing would be to cut the gores wider at the lower edge. This can be accomplished by slashing the center of each piece of skirt pattern from the hem to the seam at the waist.

Spread the pattern several inches at the hemline and taper to nothing at the waist. You may also add several inches to each side seam, beginning at the hips.

Applying Jewels

Q. I am making my daughter's wedding gown and it will be sprinkled with tiny rhinestones and pearls. Is there a way of applying them without sewing each one separately?

A. I have found that a white household glue called Sobo will do a beautiful job of holding the jewels. You must work very carefully, however, and use small tweezers to hold the jewels.

Place a little dab of glue on a jewel and stick it to the fabric. Work on only a small area at a time and allow plenty of time for the glue to dry.

Early Start Won't Affect Color of Lace and Satin

Q. I will be making the wedding gown for my future daughter-in-law. The gown is to be made of satin with a taffeta slip. Will the reembroidered lace and satin turn yellow if I begin with this big project several months ahead of the wedding date?

A. By all means, begin early—this is more work than you would imagine. The satin, taffeta and any lace you might applique on the gown will not change color in a matter of months. The color might deepen if you pack it away for twenty years or more.

When working with reembroidered lace, remember that you won't have to throw away any of this beautiful lace. You can applique any leftover lace on the veil or shoes. Simply use a loose running stitch. There is no need to overcast any of the lace edges because the embroidery keeps the lace in shape.

Gathers That Work

Q. I am making my daughter's bridesmaids' dresses and am about to tear my hair out. The skirts are very full and have three tiers of gathered sections. Each section has to be gathered

Fig. 16 — Gathers that Work

before being applied to the next one. Just about the time I have half gathered, my thread breaks and there goes my disposition. Can you suggest any tips for gathers that work?

A. Everyone faces the same problem since the gathers are certainly very popular in bridesmaids' dresses. (See figure 16.)

I would suggest using buttonhole twist or heavy-duty thread in the bobbin of the sewing machine. When stitching the gathers, place one row of stitching exactly on the seamline and the second row ¼ inch closer to the cut edge. Do not use the smallest nor the largest stitch available because you would have pleats, not nice even gathers.

When the two rows of stitching have been completed, carefully pull the two bobbin threads evenly and you will see the gathers pull up easily. Even them out so that they fit the piece of fabric to which they are to be attached.

Pin in place and machine stitch over the row of gathering thread that was exactly on the seamline. You should have perfect luck every time.

Fig. 17 – Center Front Seam

Center Front Seam

Q. I am in the process of making bridesmaids' dresses for my daughter's wedding. There is a seam directly down the center front of the dress. Perhaps it won't be as noticeable as I imagine, but I would like to eliminate this seam altogether. Would I be wrong to do this?

A. There are several reasons why there would be a seam at the center front of a garment. First, perhaps the fabric wasn't wide enough to cut without the seam. Skirts have so much more fullness than with the simple A-line dresses that, depending on the width of the fabric, perhaps a seam is necessary.

I have found, too, that when there is a seam at the center front, the seam is usually shaped. Sometimes it is indented slightly at the waist, giving it a closer fit to the body, and very often it is flared out at the hemline to help achieve the slightly wider and more flowing skirt.

I think you will normally find more garments with seams at the center front if they are cut without a waistline seam. When a waistline seam is cut into the pattern, there are other ways of gaining bodice fit and flare at the hem.

I think you will also find that the seam will not be noticed, and because of the cut of the garment, you would be unwise to eliminate it. (See figure 17.)

Should You Underline Chiffon?

Q. I will be making all of the bridesmaids' dresses for my daughter's wedding. The girls have decided on an empire style in printed polyester chiffon. My problem is whether we should underline the gowns with a solid-colored lining or they should wear slips. What do you recommend?

A. As for the construction of your bridesmaids' gowns, I usually never recommend underlining these sheers. When you do, you take away the soft, floating sheer effect of the fabric. Since you tell me the style is empire, which is above the waistline, a half-slip would never do.

I would suggest you make a separate slip-dress, which is usually fitted like a sheath dress—rather straight, with tiny shoulder straps. You would probably not want to line the sleeves.

Remember, when working with sheers, you usually double stitch the seams ⅛ inch apart and cut the excess close to the seams. You usually don't press the seams open. Also, watch the clipping and notching of fabrics.

For curves, it's better to clip the seam allowances rather close to prevent their showing through. If you need interfacing for collars and cuffs, you can use polyester chiffon. It's sheer and yet has just enough body.

Zipper on the Bias

Q. The dress pattern for my daughter's wedding gown called for the back slit to be open to almost the waist and then put together with small loops and buttons. I decided to close the back with a zipper instead. The dress is cut with the center back on the bias, and no matter what I have done, the zipper buckles. What can I do to prevent this?

A. I'm sorry, but there is no way I have ever found to successfully put a zipper in a completely bias dress without pulling. Your first clue would have been when the pattern itself had an opening with only a few loops and buttons to close part of it.

Close whatever part of the back you wish closed with the loops and tiny buttons they suggest at least to the waistline. It is not too difficult to put a seven-inch zipper in the skirt. The shorter length is more manageable.

Since the fabric of the dress will be cut on the bias and the zipper tape is on the straight, you must remember to stretch the bias seam, not ease it in. If you stretch it enough and use a featherlight zipper, you should have fairly good results with this.

Finishes for Organza

Q. I am making some organza dresses for a wedding and need guidance for the hems. I have always made the hems with additional width. When I look at the dresses that are ready-made, they have no hem at all and have a braid at the hem to make them stand out. Should I do this on my dresses?

A. The type of hem you would use depends on the cut of the skirt. When deep hems were used (and they were really beautiful), the skirts were cut straight at the hem and gathered or pleated at the waistline for the extra fullness. Today, many of the skirts are circular and, of course, the deep hems won't work.

I think where there is no hem and the hemline has shaping for a wide A-line or circle, the hair braid is applied so the skirt will stand away from the lining and not have such a limp appearance.

Narrow hair braid is available at most notion counters. Topstitch one edge of the braid to the garment, turn the braid to inside of garment and topstitch close to the edge through braid and fabric. The machine stitching is so close to the edge it is not noticeable on the right side. If necessary, you may catch stitch the free edge of the braid to the seams only.

Special Techniques for Handling Sheer Fabrics

Q. I am making a bridesmaid's dress of embroidered organdy. All the seams that have been layered, clipped or notched show through on the right side. What is the proper technique for handling sheer fabrics?

A. There is a completely different set of rules when using sheer, see-through fabrics. Instead of the clipping necessary to release extra fabric and the notching out to remove excess, you must compensate in another way.

All seams must be trimmed fairly close. Parts of the garment that will be turned (because two layers have been sewn together) must be trimmed to ⅛ inch. This will eliminate the need for clipping and notching.

Because the fabric is so sheer, you must trim these seams very evenly. They won't be noticed if you are careful. As to your regular seams, machine stitch them a second time ⅛ inch from the first stitching; then trim them close to the second stitching. These seams are usually not pressed open.

If you desire, you may use the French seaming method for sheers. However, you will usually not find this detail used in ready-to-wear.

Handling Qiana®

Q. I have questions concerning two fabrics, both made of Qiana®. The bride's gown is to be made from Qiana® satin, a beautiful woven fabric with a soft satin face. The other, for the bridesmaids, is one of Qiana® satin knit. Since this is a new fabric for me, could you give me some instructions on how to handle these fabrics, type of machine needle, stitch length and linings?

A. First, let's discuss the Qiana® satin for the bridal gown. Since this is a woven fabric, you must consider the style of garment and then decide whether you wish to underline it (treating the two layers of fabric as one).

You will use a regular machine needle, preferably a small size such as a 9 or 11. Use very fine dressmaker pins. Be sure to use a polyester thread. Satins of all types are difficult to rip (the stitches will show), so be sure to prefit the garment first; then cut it out of the Qiana®.

Since Qiana® is a nylon, your iron must not be too hot. Always press lightly on the wrong side, never so hard that it has an ironed look. Qiana®, like any luxury satin fabric, should look almost unpressed.

For the Qiana® satin knit, use ball-point machine needles and pins. This fabric may have a free-hanging lining; it is never underlined. Often, the bodice will be lined in another layer of the same fabric for compatibility. Usually, you wouldn't use lace at the hem. Instead, use Stitch Witchery, a web-type bonding, or a self-binding.

Since Qiana® knit will stretch, be careful when applying the zipper tape or it will pucker. Hair braid is used more for the hems of chiffon and organza. I don't think I would like it with Qiana® knit.

Since you are unfamiliar with both of these fabrics, it would pay you to do some test stitching and pressing to see exactly how it will handle. This extra caution could save a lot of time and money.

Chapter 17
IMPORTANT ACCESSORIES

Make Your Own Shawl

An important accessory item is the shawl or scarf. It seems that no garment is complete without one. You can wear one casually or for the most formal occasions—the fabric will dictate which it is to be.

Tartans or plaids are so popular and there are so many great selections in marvelous colors. Why not plan a skirt with a shawl? (See figure 18.)

If you want a fifty-four-inch shawl, you would purchase an extra 1½ yards of fabric, trim the square carefully, cutting all edges on a perfect grain line. Most shawls are finished by self-fringing about an inch, or contrasting your fabric with fringe that you make with yarn or a purchased fringe.

When complete, fold diagonally in half to form a triangle and casually wrap it around yourself. It's a perfect foil for those first cool days of fall.

A note on self-fringing fabric: If it's difficult to fringe your fabric, clip into the wool the desired width of finished fringe every four to six inches; then proceed to pull out these shorter length threads. The finished look will never reveal your secret.)

Cummerbunds for Tent Dresses

Q. I love the look of the wider crushed cummerbunds that are seen with the fuller tent-type dresses. My problem is that although I have a small waistline, I have a large rib cage and the belts seem to want to double over so that I can't keep them as nice and straight as they should be. Any hints?

A. You are not alone in this. Wider belts have caused many women concern unless they are absolutely flat above the waist.

Fig. 18 – Make Your Own Shawl

Let me suggest that if you use a fabric-type cummerbund, you may want to gather it in vertical lines, one at the side seams and possibly each side of the zipper. It may also be necessary to use the gathers at the side fronts as well. I have found that two rows work better than one. Then you will pull your bobbin threads until the cummerbund is the correct width.

Now, from the wrong side of your cummerbund, hand whip strips of featherboning over the vertical gathering. This will keep the gathers in place and will prevent the cummerbund from doubling over.

You might find that instead of gathers, you can lay your fabric in even folds the entire length of the belt; then tack the folds in place (as many spots as necessary). Again, hand whip the featherboning to the wrong side to hold the folds in place.

For the new obi-type belts that are wide in front and narrow at the sides, ending in a tie that continues from back and ties in front, be sure to add enough interfacing to the wide front section to keep a smooth look. Let's face it, the wider belt is not for everyone. First, decide whether it does anything for you; then adjust the type and width for your own figure.

Chiffon Scarf

Q. I followed your suggestion about making a chiffon scarf with the curled edges. You told us to cut it on the bias, which I did, but I still can't get the edges to ruffle. Any further suggestions?

A. Seems as though you are on the right track. All four edges must be cut on the bias since the fabric is woven. When finishing the edges, turn them over ¼ inch and press.

Set your sewing machine to the shortest length zigzag or satin stitch. As you stitch the hem, be sure to pull the fabric—this is what causes it to curl and ruffle. The more you pull as you stitch, the more curled it will be. The edges should look overcast.

After you have completed the machine stitching, carefully cut away the ¼ inch you turned over so that only the machine stitching is at the edges.

Hemming Scarf

Q. I'm so discouraged, I could cry. I bought several exciting scarf prints to hem. Unhappily, they aren't finished because I just couldn't do the professional edge stitching at the corners. My machine literally ate up the fabric at the corners. What can I do?

A. I love your expression about the machine "eating up the corners." It was well put.

Trying to avoid this catastrophe, my daughter Vicki came up with the greatest trick ever and wants to share it with you. I'll write the instructions in detail.

1. Prepare the scarf for machine hemming by turning over ½ inch of the four cut edges and pressing sharply.

2. Use 100 percent cotton thread in your machine if possible. It makes a much nicer edge.

3. Set your machine on a narrow zigzag stitch with a small setting so the stitches will fill in very closely.

4. Never begin at the corner, but at the center of one of the sides.

5. Cut four pieces of paper, each about two inches square.

6. As you get near a corner, slip one of the pieces of paper under the corner of the fabric so the paper extends beyond the edge of your fabric.

7. When you get near the corner, you will be stitching through the paper as well as the fabric. Because the paper is firm, it will stabilize the corners and permit you to stitch right up to the corner, turn, and continue around the corner to the next corner, until finished.

8. Carefully pull the paper from each corner and cut the excess fabric from all of the edges—close to the stitching. Stitching on this double edge makes a nicer edge. The results should be perfect every time.

Stock Tie Effect

Q. What is a stock tie effect instead of the usual bow for blouses?

A. For a wrapped or stock tie effect, you start with a tie about six inches wide. Since it is cut on the bias, you will wind up with a tie approximately three inches wide. It should be about two yards long. If your fabric is too lightweight, you might wish to line it, but I feel the width of the tie will keep it from looking skimpy.

Stitch and turn the two ends of the tie, leaving the center portion that fits the neck opening unstitched. Apply to your dress or blouse the same as any narrow tie.

To tie correctly, cross the ends at the front, wrapping each end around the neck in back and ending in the front again. Either flip the ends over as an ascot, or tie in a tight knot leaving the ends loose.

This type of neckline is very soft and flattering, but if your neck is too short, it would be too much fabric wrapped around the neck for you.

Ultrasuede® Belt

Q. I would love to have a collection of colored belts in Ultrasuede®. They make such nifty tie belts on dresses, and they aren't too costly. My problem is that when I stitch the two layers together on the cut edges, the fabric pushes forward and the stitching never looks even. Can you help?

A. Because of the nap of the Ultrasuede®, it does want to slip, especially on such a narrow strip.

First, allow at least an extra seam allowance on the width of the belt, and either fold the Ultrasuede® or use two separate cut strips.

Cut a strip of Stitch Witchery slightly smaller than the Ultrasuede®, place it between the two layers and fuse. The fusing should be done with a damp sponge on a see-through press cloth using a fairly hot iron (not the steam iron). Press by holding in position at least thirty seconds before pressing the next section.

When the entire belt has been fused, carefully machine stitch at the desired width on each side and again ¼ inch in from the first stitching. When stitching is completed, it will be simple to cut a nice straight edge very, very close to your stitching on all edges. You will find the fusing of the Ultrasuede® has prevented slippage.

Fig. 19 – Eyelet Cover-up

Eyelet Cover-Up

An eyelet shawl is simple and inexpensive to make. It's perfect for a cover-up to wear with bare-shouldered dresses. (See figure 19.)

Purchase 1¼ yards of all-over eyelet. This will make two shawls, so you may want to share the fabric with a friend. You should now have a forty-five-inch square. Fold it diagonally and cut on the foldline to get two large triangles. If you don't care for the deep triangle at the center back, round the peak off to a gentle curve. Turn over and hem the long bias edge. This can be done on the sewing machine. It is best to purchase a little extra of the preruffled eyelet trim, ranging from two to six inches wide.

On the two outer edges, turn the raw edge in about 1/4 inch and machine stitch close to the edge. Next, baste and machine stitch the finished edge of the ruffle to your shawl. It will only take minutes to make. Also, it's fresh and fun to wear, and serves the purpose as a light cover-up with glamour.

Chapter 18
CLOTHES FOR TRAVEL

Shawls Are Great

Q. I am going to a resort city soon and was wondering what type of wrap I should wear with a formal gown. Do you have any suggestions?

A. When you say "resort city," I'm sure you mean one that isn't extremely cold at night, but is too chilly to go out without a wrap. If that's the case, you're lucky—shawls are so important in fashion that a lovely, lightweight shawl could be beautiful.

One of the most attractive shawls I have seen in a long time was made from a fifty-four-inch square of lightweight jersey. It was slashed from one corner diagonally through the center of the square to about two-thirds of the way to the opposite corner. All the edges were finished with a decorative hemming stitch you would have on your sewing machine. The slit made it much easier to drape around the shoulders and tie in place.

Take a Coat-Dress

Q. I travel a lot, and think that a coat-dress would really satisfy my needs and eliminate extra clothes. What do you think?

A. You will have to be very careful with the selection of your coat-dress pattern. If you are, you will find that it will work for you.

When choosing your pattern, find one that has a little ease on it, such as soft gathered yokes front and back; a looser sleeve, either a raglan or slightly dropped; and most important, a slight chemise appearance to be belted. If you choose a pattern with a fitted waistline seam, it will be too close-fitting to wear as a coat.

When choosing the dress to wear with it, you might choose a very lightweight, soft, unconstructed fabric—perhaps a print jersey to brighten up a solid coat, or a lightweight challis, or whatever. Maybe the dress would work better if it were sleeveless.

These are all little details that you will have to think about when making your selection of fabric and pattern. Since I travel quite a bit myself, I have found this type of dress does serve many occasions and certainly does cut down on the luggage you must tote with you.

Hawaii Anyone?

Q. I expect to be going to Hawaii soon. Could you suggest what to wear on the plane, as well as a wardrobe I can make that would look perfect when I get there?

A. Lucky you! Hawaii is the most beautiful place in the world. I think my next favorite occupation would be to do public relations for Hawaii.

First, take a wardrobe with you that will please you, and forget conformity. I've noticed that women around the world travel with their favorite type clothes and colors. You must try to carefully plan your wardrobe so that each major part of an ensemble can serve many occasions—don't be saddled down with too many clothes. If your trip is like most of them, you'll be island hopping and want to enjoy every minute outdoors, not inside pressing and packing.

A major item for the trip over as well as when you get there is an all-purpose coat, either a printed cotton or chintz (prints show fewer spots) or a color that coordinates with the rest of your wardrobe. Be sure your coat is lightweight and colorful, as nothing is gloomier than a drab coat on a cloudy day, and it does rain a little every day in Hawaii.

Keep everything casual, using knits and cottons. Remember, it's very hot and often humid, and heavy polyester knits would be most uncomfortable. A blazer or shirt jacket is a must. It can be worn with skirts, dresses and pants, day or evening when a light cover-up is needed.

For the beaches, I found a long wrap skirt in a lightweight knit tricot the greatest item I had with me. Everyone wanders from the beaches right to the shops on the main streets, and then into restaurants and hotels. The skirt can change your swim suit instantly and be acceptable anywhere. At the same time, you might consider a white eyelet or cotton lace shirt. It can be worn over a swimsuit, or with shirts or pants, and double as a lightweight cover-up for long evening dresses.

For daytime or evening, remember one thing—keep your clothes colorful and casual, and you'll join the fun and look like you belong in this true paradise.

Spain Tour

Q. My husband and I are going on a tour of Spain for about ten days this spring, and since this is our first trip, we don't know what kind of clothes to wear. Can you help us pack the right clothes with the least amount of luggage?

A. You tell me you are going to Spain in the spring. This could mean cold and warm weather, so you must be prepared for both. Therefore, the layered look is the most satisfactory. Since you will be packing a limited wardrobe, spend lots of time coordinating your wardrobe so that every piece will mix and match.

Usually a tour such as the one you describe is not the type where very dressy clothes are needed. You will probably start out in the morning and not arrive back at your hotel until late in the evening, so don't plan to change clothes several times a day.

Since your wardrobe will be limited, plan on beautiful colors to keep from feeling drab. Scarfs and blouses add a great relief of color and can make any garment more attractive.

First, plan a jacket ensemble, either a blazer jacket or a shirt jacket combined with a skirt or jumper and blouses or sweaters, for quick changes. With the jacket, plan pants—they are accepted everywhere and are the most comfortable for travel.

A jumper dress or tunic top that can be worn with or without a blouse serves a dual purpose. Combine a long skirt that will coordinate with your blouses, sweaters, and jacket. A long skirt can be very tailored but give just the amount of glamour you need occasionally to boost your spirits.

Naturally, you will need an all-weather coat, one that can be worn over your jacket or with a dress or pants. Try to find one with a zip-in lining for extra warmth. If you plan to take a swimsuit, take a cover-up caftan that can double as a robe worn around your hotel room and also over your swimsuit.

If possible, plan to take only one bag plus a makeup bag. You may have to carry your luggage at some unexpected time, so be prepared.

Chapter 19
NOTIONS

The subject of notions is a very wide field to cover. Here, I have merely touched on the few notion items that I have found to be invaluable. There are many manufacturers who distribute items that are very similar to the ones I have described. You will have to test other brands and be your own judge as to quality.

There are also many sewing notions flooding the market that are totally unnecessary; however, if you are a gadget freak, you probably will invest in many that are not really usable.

In this section, I have described items that I personally use and recommend. As the world of fabrics widens and fashions change, it is only natural that we will always have new sewing aids.

Tape-Stitch By Belding

With so much topstitching used in today's fashions, tape-stitch is a precise guide for perfectly even stitching. Never stitch through tape-stitch; instead place it on your fabric (it sticks) as a guide, with the edge of the tape just inside the line for the machine stitching. The tape also has perforations that can be clipped for curves. You will find many uses for this fine product. It's a guide for handpicking, for stitching and placing zippers, and for marking grain line on suedes and vinyls. You may also place a strip of it on the sole plate of your sewing machine as a seam guide.

Fashion Ruler By Fashionetics

This is a clear, transparent ruler that combines the French curve, armhole and hip curve. It also has a cut-out slot to control tracing wheel or seam markings. A splendid accessory!

Lint Brush

Did you know that if you blow the lint out of your machine and bobbin case, your saliva can add just enough moisture to corrode the metal parts? Always keep the needle area and bobbin case clean by brushing with your lint brush.

Roller Foot By Belding-Lily

This will reduce skipping stitches on knits when all else fails. It reduces the uneven feed, works for leathers and vinyls and many hard-to-sew fabrics.

Pins

My very favorite pins are called IRIS and are made in Switzerland. These super fine, long silk pins have finally become available in this country. The length of the pins keeps them from slipping out of spongy fabrics and they can still be used for the finest silks. You'll love them!

Needle-Lube

This is a new product that prevents skipped stitches. It also prevents friction heat on heavy materials, although it is made especially for knits and sheer materials. It lubricates the thread guide and tension, preventing thread drag while sewing knits. It can be used for hand sewing, too. It also lubricates scissors. We've tried it and it does work.

Dritz® Point Turner

This little plastic gadget turns collar points without poking holes in the corners. It can be used to remove basting stitches because of the point. It also has a neat design that allows it to slip around a button as you sew the button on, forming a button shank.

Bound Buttonhole Maker By Dritz®

If you have trouble making bound buttonholes (and they are returning in better read-to-wear), this little gadget is your answer. It helps you stitch those fine little welts evenly whether they are cut on the bias or straight. The stitching is always even, starting and stopping at exactly the same spot, almost foolproof!

Skirt Marker By Scovil

With a firm, tripod base, this is used with pins for accuracy. Almost everyone can mark a hem for you accurately with this gadget. Yes, even husbands!

Stay-Lastic

Stay-Lastic is elastic cord by Scoville. It is a nice, heavy elastic cord that can be used for stabilizing waistlines. It is stronger and more versatile than elastic thread, which should only be used for gathering.

Nonroll Elastic

Nonroll elastic is for waistbands in skirts, slacks, and shorts. This is a firm, medium-weight elastic that resists rolling or twisting. It comes in ¾ and one-inch widths. Be sure the package clearly states nonroll. There are several brands available.

Sewing Gauge By Dritz®

The sewing gauge is a handy, double-pointed metal slider with the new metric measures as well as the conventional measurements. It is only six inches long, and I have found it to be one of the handiest items in my sewing box. It's perfect for marking hem depth, spacing of buttonholes and buttons, marks, tucks and pleats—a real must!

Shoulder Pads By E. Z. Buckle Company

It's just in time for all those new patterns that call for a lightweight shoulder pad. This lightweight shoulder pad is completely washable and dry-cleanable. Covered in acetate rayon, it's perfect to insert in dresses, blouses, and unlinded jackets.

Tape-Measure By Dritz®

This is called the super-glo. It is a waterproof no-stretch vinyl tape measure with metrics on one side.

Tack-It

Tack-it is a neat pattern marker that marks both layers of fabric. It uses transfer paper. It has easy-to-follow instructions. You'll become addicted to this gadget in a hurry.

Tracing Wheels

I won't go into this item because I have seen too many disastrous results from the markings showing through on some fabrics, which are often impossible to remove. It can be used successfully if you test the fabric and make sure it will work. I personally have used other ways of marking fabric more successfully.

Seam Ripper

Handle this item cautiously. I'm not in favor of it except to pick up threads to be pulled for ripping. I don't like a ripper for actually ripping seams—a slip of your hand and you've sliced into your fabric. Use this gadget with great care and respect.

Loop-Turner By Dritz®

This product is perfect for turning bias tubing, button loops, shoulder straps, string belts, and spaghetti trim.

Beeswax and Holder By Dritz®

Run your hand sewing thread through this gadget. It strengthens the thread and stabilizes it to prevent tangling. It also has several household uses as described on the package.

Hook and Eye Closures By Dritz®

This is a large, flat hook and eye that is perfect for pants and skirts. They are easy to sew on. They prevent tearing of fabric that usually occurs when using the very small hooks and eyes.

Buttonhole Cutter

A buttonhole cutter is a small square wood block plus a sharp chisel blade on a handle. It's perfect for cutting open machine buttonholes sharply and cleanly, without any danger of cutting too far or leaving any ragged edges. This gadget is available, to my knowledge, only through your Bernina® sewing machine dealer. It's worth its weight in gold!

Double-Needle By Risdon

You use this for decorative stitching where two rows of even stitching are desired. This works best on straight areas such as jacket front, hems, and cuffs.

Yellow Band By Singer

This ball-point needle is for stitching knits. It gives more thread control if you are having difficulty sewing with a regular ball-point needle. Check size and type of needle before using.

Home Repair Needles By Belding

This package is invaluable for every household. It has a variety of unusual needles, including carpet needle, awning or tent needle, upholsters, car seat, glovers' needle, and mattress needle. These are designed to reach hard-to-get spots and to accommodate unusual fabrics that simply wouldn't work with regular needles.

Hand Sewing Needles

I prefer the English needles for strength and perfection. An average size for most projects is a size 8, and an average type for most uses is a long-eyed needle called crewel embroidery by Coats or Belding.

BETWEENS have a smaller eye and are a very short needle, wonderful for padding stitches in tailoring. SHARPS are a long needle with a small eye. If you sew a lot, you will want a complete collection of hand sewing needles, both in size and type. I have only singled out one type of needle for the average person who doesn't do much sewing.

Iron-All

Iron-all is a shield for your iron that makes it safe to press all fabrics. Its tiny perforations distribute steam evenly over the surface of your fabric. It can also be used on napped fabrics such as corduroy. It prevents scorching and can be used for applying press-on interfacings.

Press-Cloths By Dritz®

Vue-Thru is a sheer, see-through press cloth for light pressing. I also feel you need the chemically treated press-cloth by Dritz® that is made in a heavy duck fabric. I prefer this for pressing heavier fabrics where additional moisture is required. Moisten this cloth with a wet sponge and use a hotter iron to create more steam.

Point-Presser

A point-presser is a wooden board with an exposed or raised long narrow area for pressing all seams open after stitching.

Pounding Block

Use a pounding block for forcing steam out of a pressed area.

Pressing Ham

Use a pressing ham for shaping curves areas. The three items mentioned above are available separately by June Tailor Pressing Aids.

Tailor Trix Board

A combination board that incorporates all of the pressing equipment into one is the Tailor Trix Board available only through Eunice Farmer.

Scissors

There are literally hundreds of scissors on the market. Many of them aren't worth a bargain price or any price. I am in favor of purchasing the finest scissors you can buy and keep them for SEWING ONLY. No scissors will be usable if you use them to cut paper, cardboard and various and sundry household items. For serious dressmaking and tailoring, I prefer two sizes of scissors. I like a five- or six-inch sewing scissors (one point is heavier than the other for strength) for all clipping and cutting threads. For cutting fabric, I prefer the eight- or nine-inch bent shears, Gingher or Wiss. If treated with respect, they will last for years. I'm still using the same shears I used twenty years ago.

If you have arthritis in your hands or simply can't use a heavier shears, get the plastic-handled scissors. However, don't expect them to give the same service that heavier metal shears give.

Make a Lapboard

If you haven't known the luxury of a lapboard, you just haven't lived. It is a portable table you can keep near your sewing machine. Put it on your lap and you immediately have a nice level surface for pinning your fabric or whatever. (See figure 20.)

It also serves in many ways for everyone in the family. It's perfect for playing cards and for someone in bed to use to work puzzles, eat, or write letters. Perhaps you will know many more uses for this fabulous gadget that belongs in every household.

It just occurred to me that with all the workshop tools your husbands have, I'm sure you won't have any difficulty getting one made. The lapboard is made of ¼-inch masonite, smooth on one side. See the sketch for a more accurate picture.

We have had many gals come up with great ideas for making the lap board more usable. You can add a self-sticking tape measure to the top of the board and a pin cushion. You'll have a pin cushion that won't roll off onto the floor.

Depending on just how many uses you will need, you can think of other innovations that will make it just perfect for your needs.

The first time I saw a lapboard was in my grandmother's home. She brought it to this country from Switzerland. It's not new at all, but it is surprisingly new to most women. You'll love it!

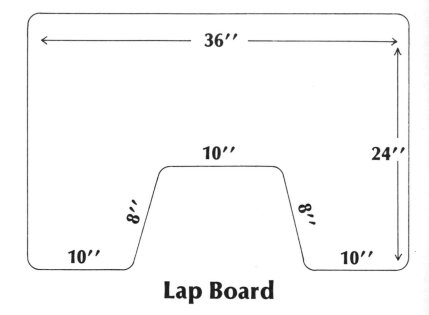

Fig. 20 – Make a Lap Board

Lap Board

Pattern Adjuster

A handy visual aid for making pattern alterations and adjustments on commercial patterns as well as an aid for designing your own patterns is a cutting board called the Adjuster by E. Z. Buckle Company. It has a graduation of sizes for bodice and skirts for sizes six to twenty so you can immediately find the difference between sizes and alter your pattern to fit.

The board also shows where to measure the bust and the hips for adjustments, and has guidelines for bias, French curves, scallops and other techniques. Measurements are in both inches and metric units.

Trace a Pattern

Here's a product to use when preserving patterns or designing or altering them. It's called Trace a Pattern and is made by the Stacy Company. It's inexpensive, strong, transparent, sheer and has a web-like appearance.

Trace a Pattern can be used to duplicate your favorite pattern, alter patterns or make adjustments in them. Place it over ready-made garments and you can immediately see the grain line, the outline of the garment, and come up with a workable pattern to copy.

To make a sample pattern to check for fit before cutting into expensive fabric, machine stitch on Trace a Pattern with a long stitch that can be easily removed. When adjustments have been made, you can actually use the Trace a Pattern for cutting the fabric.

This is only the beginning. I'm sure you will find many other uses for this product.

Basting Tape

A product I want you to be aware of is Basting Tape by Talon. This is a roll of double-faced adhesive tape that often eliminates pinning and basting.

Basting Tape is perfect for zipper applications. Simply apply to the front edges of the zipper tape, finger press the zipper to seam allowances and machine stitch. It also stabilizes zipper to fabric, eliminating slippage and puckering. However, you should NEVER machine stitch through the tape.

It can be used to position pockets or trims before stitching. It's perfect for matching stripes and plaids. If you are craft-minded, it is perfect for affixing paper, felt and other lightweight materials used in craft projects.

Hemming Clips

I never write about any product or gadget without thoroughly testing it in our own sewing classes. Students are our severest critics. One gadget I think deserves merit is a package with six hemming clips.

Often disappointment and desperation come with the first fitting of a garment. This is true in part because the garment is still in the unfinished state and because of the length, which you have done nothing about.

Turn up a hem on the hemline of the pattern as a guide and use your hemming clips to hold it in place. The clips won't leave marks and are especially good on fabrics that can't be pinned or where chalk won't show.

When you try your garment on, you will have some idea of the way it will look when completed. The clips can be easily slipped off when it's time for an accurate length to be taken.

Hemming clips are made by Risdon and can be found at almost all notion departments.

You might want two packages for you'll find many more uses for them than I have mentioned. They also can be used to hold leather, fake fur, and other fabrics that aren't pinned while you are constructing your garment.

Magnetic Seam Guide

With the high cost of ready-to-wear, each and every day we have many new home sewers. One of the most difficult of all details for a beginning sewer to learn is to stitch accurate seams. Unless you have a calibrated eye that never fails, there is a gadget that I can't stress strongly enough for everyone—a magnetic seam guide.

You don't have to screw it in place; just slide it onto your machine to whatever width seam you will be stitching. It also works on curves and it's a great aid for topstitching. When you don't need it, just slide it out of the way (being magnetic, it won't fall off and get lost).

The brand I am referring to is made by Belding. However, I am sure there are others that will work equally well. Try it—you'll never want to be without one.

Body Suits Made Easy

Another great product on the market is called Snap-ease, which converts blouses, shirts and tops into a body suit. Snap-ease is made of fine nylon tricot with a snap crotch, elastic legs, and three sizes: small, medium and large.

Best of all, they can be applied in minutes with a simple hand or machine stitch. This is great for the gal who doesn't have time to make her own body suit and doesn't like blouses that bulge and pop out from pants and skirts.

You can also use any dress pattern and convert it to a blouse by cutting it to hip length and adding your snap-ease. You'll find all the instructions included in each package. I hope you like them as much as I do.

Tissue Tape

Tissue Tape by Belding prevents slippage. Unlike the sticking tape that guides ornamental topstitching, this nonsticking Tissue Tape is for plain, basic stitching of seams when the difficult material is likely to slip, stretch, creep, or snag.

The Tissue Tape can be pinned over the seamline, and knit, sheers and open weaves (including laces, pile fabrics, velvets) are easily stitched. There are guidelines for seam stitching with the seam allowances clearly marked.

When stitching is completed, the tape is gently pulled off in large strips, leaving no tiny tissue specks to bother with. With today's new fabrics, you will find many other ingenious uses for this Tissue Tape.

Proper Needles

Q. Why do you say we should never use ball-point needles for woven fabrics? I have used them with no problem.

A. You've been lucky!

A ball-point needle is designed for knits because its rounded point allows it to find its way between ribs of the knit without piercing the threads which could cause a snag.

A regular machine needle is so sharp and fine that it is preferred for woven fabrics because it will go right through a slub or weave of the fabric without causing it to pull. They are both different and it is recommended that you use them accordingly.

When working with silks or very fine woven fabrics, it is important to replace your sewing machine needle often. Use a very fine point such as a size 9 to prevent pulling those fine, fine threads. The proper needle can make all the difference in your machine stitching, and I would certainly recommend you use the needles the experts advise.

Quality Thread

Q. My question concerns thread. Many authorities recommend sewing with cotton thread, and some say to use silk. What kind of thread do you suggest?

A. There are so many threads on the market today—some of them are excellent, others are not as satisfactory. I have found that the 100 percent long staple polyester fibers work perfectly.

We have had excellent results with a thread called Metrosene, made in Switzerland. It is available in most better stores and can be used on cottons, silks, and polyesters with great success. It doesn't break, ball up, or split as easily as cotton-polyester blends.

Naturally, I haven't used every type of thread, but I do know that Belding is also a very reputable thread on the market. Once you find one that works for you, stick with it. I don't feel that silk or cotton thread is necessary.

Buttonhole Twist

Q. My question concerns the use of buttonhole twist thread in my sewing machine. I have so much difficulty with the stitches. The lengths seem to vary, the thread breaks and all sorts of frustrating things happen. Is there a secret? When do you advise using this heavy thread?

A. Buttonhole twist thread does cause difficulty for most women because of the thickness of the thread and the sensitivity of sewing machines.

You will have to experiment with your own sewing machine. Some of them will take this heavy thread in the top with regular thread for the bobbin while others will take the buttonhole twist in the top and the bobbin. You will always need a larger needle than you ordinarily use, probably a size 16.

Before you give up altogether, you might decide if this is actually the thread you want to use. Today, with so many garments topstitched as a fashion detail, you may not need the heavier thread.

Seams, hems, all outer edges and every possible detail is machine topstitched today. Simply use the same length stitch and your regular thread and you will have perfect results (stitching at least two rows about ¼ inch apart).

I would only recommend buttonhole twist as a thread for sewing on buttons, handpicking zippers or making thread loops for buttons or belt carriers. If you are making a coat of cashmere or camel's hair, you can use buttonhole twist and handpick all the outer edges to keep them flat and add a decorative touch.

Buttonhole Twist for Gathering

Q. Can you use buttonhole twist for gathering stitches?

A. Because of the strength of buttonhole twist, I recommend using it on your bobbin when stitching two rows of stitches that will be pulled up for a gathered effect. The most maddening thing I know of is to pull yards of fabric up for gathers and then, before you are finished, having the thread break. Because of buttonhole twist's extra strength, it will not break, thus preventing a few unhappy moments.

Short Zippers

Q. Have the zipper companies stopped making five- and six-inch zippers? So many patterns call for the shorter zippers, and yet they simply can't be found in the notion counters.

A. This length zipper is usually confined to the manufacturers since they are very limited in demand. However, it is quite simple to adjust the length of a zipper to suit your particular needs.

There are two ways that this can be done. The first is to mark the zipper tape at the length you desire. Hand sew back and forth across the teeth of the zipper at this point.

As a safeguard, you might even sew a narrow piece of tape across this point as well as hand sewing across the zipper teeth to prevent the key of the zipper from coming off the cut end.

Cut off the excess length of the zipper about one inch beyond the desired length.

A safer way to adjust the length of the zipper would be to apply the zipper to your garment, allowing the excess length to extend above the waistline of your finished garment.

Machine stitch the waistband on the garment, stitching across the teeth of the zipper. Cut off the excess length, again, allowing about one inch above the cut.

Since the waistband has been machine stitched in position, the zipper cannot run off the end of the tape.

Actually, it is so simple to adjust the length of a zipper that you will find if you stock up on a few basic sizes, they can be shortened to any length you desire very easily and quickly.

Fig. 21 – Velcro® for a Wrap-around Skirt

Velcro® for Wraparound Skirt

Q. I dislike the long ties that are so often found on wraparound skirts. Is there any way I could apply Velcro® to my skirt, or would the weight of the skirt be too much strain on the Velcro® to keep it closed?

A. Velcro® is a trade name for one of the most wonderful inventions of all time. Thank goodness we are finding more and more uses for it.

For those of you who are unfamiliar with it, Velcro® is made of two strips of tape that have hundreds of tiny hooks and loops that actually lock together tightly the instant you press them together, yet they peel apart easily.

It is lightweight, nonjamming and easy to align, and would be perfect for wrap skirts. It also

152

works perfectly for other skirts and pants—eliminating hooks, snaps or buttons on waistbands.

When constructing a waistband to use with Velcro®, you must allow several extra inches to extend beyond the center front or center back on the side of the waistband that will be under the top or finished edge of the waistband.

This will not show because you will apply two inches of Velcro® to the inside of the waistband and it will lap over the extension of the waistband where you will add another two inches of tape. Simply press them together. It really works beautifully. (See figure 21.)

Washing Velcro®

Q. My problem is that when I wash a garment that has a Velcro® fastener, it pulls and tears any other fabric in the washer. Is there a way to avoid this?

A. Yes. Always close the fastener. This will prevent the tiny synthetic teeth from gripping onto any other fabric. If you close it properly, there is no way it can separate during washing.

Scotchgard®

Q. Is it safe to use spray Scotchgard® (a product of Minnesota Mining and Manufacturing Company) on the underarm part of a garment?

A. Yes, it is possible to use Scotchgard® on just about any fabric if you carefully read the directions on the can. I have personally used it and recommended it on fabrics such as silks for wedding gowns, bridesmaids' dresses and such where nerves can play a big part in bringing on perspiration where it was never a problem before.

Because everyone has a different interpretation of directions and the application of products, I would strongly recommend you always try the spray on a piece of the same fabric before you spray it on a finished garment. Often it is necessary to spray it twice lightly instead of one heavy spraying that might actually cause spotting. This is a wonderful product and we have found many uses for it, including spraying a new tie for the men in your life. You'd be surprised how easy it is to wipe off spots that seem to come from nowhere.

Scotchgard® and Polyester

Q. My problem is the perspiration stains and odor that linger on double knit clothes. My friends seem to have the same problem. Do you have a solution for removing or lessening the stains and odor?

A. If the climate is excessively hot and humid where you live, you should try to find knits that are made of cotton instead of polyester (or a blend of fibers). One hundred percent polyesters don't breathe and are hot and clammy to wear, and will retain odors longer than other fibers.

The obvious answer is to try to prevent the perspiration in the first place by using a deodorant often. You may find it necessary to try several of them before finding one that works for you.

Try spraying new fabrics with Scotchgard®. You may spray twice at the underarm area.

I know that this will work on almost all fabrics and will prevent perspiration from soaking into the fabrics. This works beautifully for anyone who is under a nervous strain and the perspiration problem pops up.

Sorry about clothes that already have the stain and odor, but it usually can't be eliminated once it is there. You may try soaking your clothes in a solution of baking soda, but this is no guarantee. You must try to prevent this from happening in the first place.

Tapes and Bindings

Q. There are so many different types of sewing tapes and bindings on the store shelves that it becomes confusing. Could you explain the major differences and the main purpose of each type?

A. The reason there are many new types of tapes is because there are new fabrics that require different features. For example, if your fabric is a stretch fabric, you would use stretch lace or bias tape for your hem. In knits or fabrics that don't ravel, I usually don't recommend any finish at the hem.

For woven fabrics, you can still use the lace as well as the woven hem tape. Both are compatible with the nonstretch fabric. A good point to remember is not to change the flexibility of the fabric. If it is a stretch fabric, all bindings must have a stretch quality.

Bias tape is used more as a binding for outer edges than it is for seam finishings. However, for unlined jackets it's very professional to enclose the seams, including armhole seams, in the foldover bias tape. This avoids raveling and raw edges and gives your garment a custom finish.

Experiment with all the new bindings. There is a whole new world of them to go along with the whole new world of fabrics.

Chapter 20
SEWING FOR HOME DECORATING

Floor Pillows

Q. I want to make some floor pillows for gifts. Would you give me some ideas about size and fabric suggestions?

A. Floor pillows are fabulous gifts and are great for just about everyone on your list. (See figure 22.)

Fabric possibilities are unlimited: You could make them out of corduroy, printed chintz, wool plaid or any textured wool, velveteen, fake fur or heavy upholstery fabrics.

As to size, I think they should be quite large—about twenty-seven to thirty square inches. Often, the width of the fabric and the amount of money you care to spend have some bearing on the measurement, but please don't make them too small or they can't be used to sit on comfortably.

It is recommended that you make an inner pillow out of muslin; then stuff it very tightly with polyester stuffing. You won't need to apply a zipper to your inner pillow.

For the outer fabric, cut it to fit the inner pillow snugly, and apply the zipper for easy removal before you machine stitch the pillow together. If the outer pillow appears too loose, you can easily turn it inside out and make your seams a little deeper.

Usually, floor pillows don't have piped or corded edges, but you can add decorative braid or fringe.

Pillows' Square Corners

Q. I started making pillows for gifts. My problem with them was never solved. When the finished pillows were stuffed, my nice square corners no longer looked square. Instead, the pillows poked out at all the corners and almost looked like they curved in at the sides. What in the world am I doing wrong?

A. This is a common fault of just about all the pillows I have ever seen. The problem is with your nice square corners. On your next, pillow, try making the seam deeper at the corners and don't stitch them square. Instead, make them slightly oval at the corners. You will find that when these have been stuffed, they will look much more square than your original pillows did. Try one and experiment to see just how much deeper to sew the corners; I would say not quite ½ inch in from the original marks.

Fig. 22 – Floor Pillows

Cotton Napkins

Q. One of my favorite gifts is napkins out of gay cotton fabrics. My problem is hemming around the corners. When I turn the corner, the machine literally eats them up and the corners are never nice and square and even. What technique would help me?

A. First, never begin hemming at the corner itself; always begin several inches from the corner. I place a piece of typing paper or wax paper under the corners, just extending the paper about one inch on each side of the corner. When you get to the corner, simply leave the needle down in the fabric, lift the presser foot, and pivot the corner.

The paper under the fabric will allow you to continue sewing without the fabric getting tangled up and drawn into the throat plate, causing it to knot up. After the hemming is completed, just carefully tear the paper away from the back of the fabric.

Overcast Edges for Napkins

Q. I can't seem to get the nice overcast edge on my chintz napkins with my machine. My edge is stretched and straggly. Have you any suggestions for this seemingly simple task?

A. All sewing machines are not capable of doing the kind of hem you are referring to, as these are done by commercial-type sewing machines. You can come up with a close second.

I recommend folding over less than ½ inch of all the outer edges and pressing carefully, being sure not to stretch the edge. Now, use your fine overcast stitch and stitch on the outer folded edge. If this is done with a close enough stitch, you should be able to cut off the excess raw edge very close to the stitching. You will have just about the same effect as the commercial machines. It will withstand many washings and not ravel loose.

If you purchase a good quality chintz, the kind used in expensive napkins, I have figured that you can make six napkins from one yard of fabric at a cost of about eighty cents each. This is a good savings, and besides, you select the perfect color and design for your home.

Make a Round Tablecloth

For outdoor casual living, Christmas, or gift giving, the round tablecloth is a perfect choice. This is a delightful way to cheer up any party for family or friends.

Before you select your fabric, you might consider coordinating a square cloth to place over the round one, as well as napkins and large and small pillows for furniture. With a little work, you can transform an ordinary scene into one that looks like the magazines.

For a floor-length round tablecloth, you must take your table measurements, both the width and the drop from table to floor or whatever length you desire. Since this will vary with the individual, our example will be for a table twenty-four inches wide, so you must change your measurements according for your own table. For this size table, you will need 4-2/3 yards of fabric forty-five inches wide.

If your table is twenty-four inches wide and you desire a thirty-inch drop, the total width will be eighty-four inches. Thus, you will need a circle of fabric this large. Since fabric doesn't come this wide, you must piece the fabric; in this case, you will need two strips of forty-five-inch fabric, each 2-1/3 yards long.

One full width of your fabric runs the entire center of the table to the floor without a seam. The second long piece of fabric is cut in half lengthwise, and each piece is stitched in a seam to the center panel. These seams will fall in folds in the finished tablecloth and not be noticed. (One point to remember: If your fabric is a plaid or has a matching pattern, you might need a little extra fabric for matching.)

After the seams have been stitched and pressed open, fold the large square of fabric into fourths. Use a measuring tape or tie a string forty-two inches long to a piece of chalk or pencil for marking fabric. Hold the string at the center fold, make a circle like a compass and mark the circle for cutting. Cut and finish the cut edges, either with a small hem, decorative lace or tape, or a zigzag finish. Presto, it's finished!

You can often make small napkins with the fabric left at the corners. If you wish to make a square cloth to place on top of the circle, which incidentally, is decorative as well as practical, usually a forty-five-inch square is ample; thus, you would need only 1¼ yards of forty-five-inch fabric for the top cloth.

You might want to coordinate pillows. You can cover lamp shades, screens, and many, many things for a true decorator touch. Do it; it's fun!

Tablecloth Edges

Q. When I tried to do the satin stitch for the edges of my circular full-length tablecloth, they weren't nice and flat, but instead, were very ripply and almost looked ruffled. How can I keep these edges nice and smooth like the ones that are ready-made?

A. If you are fortunate enough to have a sewing machine with a special foot for satin stitching that has a small hole in it for extra heavy thread (like buttonhole twist) to feed through as you do your stitching, it works perfectly.

Before you begin, however, you must turn over about ½ inch and press this fold carefully, being sure not to stretch the fabric. A circle is completely on the bias, so you must handle it extra cautiously.

If you don't have this special foot with the hole for the heavier thread to feed in as you stitch, you can do the same thing by holding the extra thread in place as you stitch. After you have stitched about ten or twelve inches, carefully pull the corded thread slightly so that any stretching disappears (be sure not to pull this thread too tight or it will cup at the hem). Then continue doing the same thing until you have finished the entire circle.

Now, VERY carefully, slip your scissors under the fold of extra fabric and cut it as close as possible to your machine stitching. Be sure not to cut the right side of the fabric. I always find that the satin stitch done on the fold is much nicer than trying to do it on a single layer of fabric. It takes a little practice, so I would experiment with a scrap of fabric cut in a circle before you begin with your tablecloth.

Bedspread Cording

Q. I need help with cording. I am making a bedspread with boxed corners. When I apply the cording to one side of the fabric, it looks smooth. When I join the second piece of fabric, it is never flat. The stitching isn't close enough to the cording. Can you help?

A. The cording should be applied the same, whether you are making pillows, spreads, or a garment for yourself. If you follow my instructions carefully, you should have perfect results every time.

Cording should be covered with the same fabric as your spread, or a contrast if desired. However, it must be cut on the bias. Be sure when stitching it close to the cording that you keep the bias even or you will end up with diagonal wrinkles.

Cut the excess fabric from the covered cord to a seam allowance of ⅝ inch. Place the cording on one section of the spread (or one section of your garment), keeping the cut edges of the seam extension of the bias even with the cut edge of the garment. Pin or baste in place and machine stitch on the same stitching you had on the cording.

It is a good idea to use the cording or zipper foot for this so that you can get very close to the cord itself. This stitching will later be your stitching guide for the final steps, so be sure it is accurate.

Lastly, place the second section of your spread (or garment) over the first, right sides together, with the seam extending. Pin from the side where you can already see the row of machine stitching where you stitched the cording to the first section.

The final step is to machine stitch over your first stitching. Again, be sure to use the cording foot. If your stitching is accurate, you should have beautiful results, with no guesswork involved.

Dust Ruffles

Q. In your opinion, what is the easiest way to make a dust ruffle that will hang nice and straight all the time?

A. The simplest way to make a dust ruffle would be to attach it to a flat sheet the exact size of your bed. Put it on the bed and measure the length of the ruffle carefully. After it is completed, it will be a joy to you because it will always stay in exactly the same position under the mattress.

Decorate Wall with Fabric

Q. I have inquired at all our local stores about a special paste for fabrics used in decorating walls, but no one seems to know about this paste. Please explain further. Also, what fabrics can be successfully used for decorating walls?

A. Perhaps if you had explained that you needed a wallpaper paste suitable for fabrics, your local shop could have helped you. There isn't a package marked for fabric only. It must be nonstaining, clear cellulose paste.

I'm sure there are many brands that fill these requirements. However, one brand that I have used is called Supercel.

I have personally used fabrics on walls for years. They are delightful and much easier to apply than paper. You can coordinate your pillows, spread, tablecloths, and drapes with one or more accent walls.

You put the paste on the wall, not the fabric. Usually the mixture should be slightly thicker than for paper. If a little gets on your fabric, you can wipe it off instantly without leaving a mark.

Almost any fabric could be used—cottons or cotton blends are perhaps best. I have used Gloria Vanderbilt chintz and handscreened cottons from Florida. If you are in doubt, you may have to purchase a small piece of fabric and experiment.

I might pass along a tip I found helpful. Instead of trying to trim the fabric exactly even at the ceiling and baseboard, leave some extra until it has dried. Then, mark the cutting line, pull the fabric back so you can cut it evenly, repaste and pat the edges in place. Fabric does have a tendency to shrink, so allow a little extra for all edges and trim when dry.

Fabric Bubbles

Q. My fabric on my walls has dried and it looks slightly bubbly. Any suggestions?

A. I can think of only one thing that might cause your trouble—did you preshrink your fabric? If you did, the fabric would not shrink a second time and when it dried, it would remain the same size.

You might have to experiment with a little less paste and spend more time smoothing the fabric with a roller. Also, whenever I have papered with fabric, I've actually lapped the seams slightly at first. Then when the fabric is dry thoroughly, I pull it back on all the seams, trim it so the seams will just butt together, repaste, and it is perfect every time.

Quilted Place Mats

Q. I am making some quilted place mats that are in an oval shape and have bias binding around the edges. When I have purchased these in the past and washed them, the edges became so tight that the place mats became all bunchy in the center. I don't want that to happen to mine. Can you give me a helpful hint about the bias?

A. The place mats bunched up at the center because the bias strip was pulled too tight when it was applied to the edges. You will be working with outer curves on your mats. As you pin the bias in place, be sure to ease it slightly, especially on the curves. Because it has been cut on the bias, the strips will ease nicely without gathers.

It might take a little practice to ease just the right amount, but you will know if you have eased too much because it will begin to look gathered. You might want to try a sample first, and then actually wash your sample before completing your project.

Bias Tape Application

Q. I'm a "bias tape freak." How in the world can I get one machine stitching to catch both sides of the tape?

A. Press the center crease from the prefolded tape and refold, making one side ⅛ inch wider—voilà, it works. Remember, when cutting and pressing your own bias strips to be folded, press the fold slightly off center.

While we're on the subject of bias tape, may I also remind you to EASE the bias when going around outer curves to avoid a bubbly look near the corners. The only time you pull the tape slightly is when you are applying to an inner curve such as a neck edge or armholes.

If you are unable to locate any of the notion items mentioned at stores in your area, please write direct to Eunice Farmer, 9814 Clayton Road, St. Louis, Missouri 63124.